WINGS OVER THE PRAIRIE

Canvasback Against the Sun, February 1979. Egg tempera on gesso board, 60.9cm x 45.7cm (24 in x 18 in)

Essays by
H. Albert Hochbaum

Compiled and edited by
George Hochbaum

Photographs by
Jack A. Barrie and
Glenn D. Chambers

Wings Over The Prairie

TAMOS Books Inc.

"April Evening" is adapted from
Travels and Traditions of Waterfowl,
H.A. Hochbaum (University of
Minnesota Press), with permission of
the University of Minnesota Press.

ISBN 1-895569-16-8

Design by A.O.Osen.

Printed in Canada.

For Tim and Flick.

Photography credits
Jack A. Barrie, 52, 53, 54, 56, 57, 60, 62-3,
69, 79, 92, 94, 96, 108, 109
Glenn D.Chambers, 16-7, 20, 25, 26, 27,
28, 29, 32, 33, 35, 36, 37, 38, 39, 42, 43,
44, 46, 47, 49, 50, 66, 73, 74, 75, 76, 78, 80
81, 84, 91, 93, 97, 99, 101, 104, 105, 106
David H. Ellis/Bruce Coleman Inc., NY, 86
Painting, p2, and pen and ink illustrations
Hans Albert Hochbaum

Canadian Cataloguing in Publication Data
Hochbaum, Hans Albert (Hans Albert), 1911–1988
    Wings over the prairie
    ISBN 1-895569-16-8

1. Ducks–North America. 2. Waterfowl–North America.
I. Hochbaum, George Sutton. 1946–ΙΙ. Barrie, Jack A.
III. Chambers, Glenn D. IV. Title.
QL696.A52H63 1993   598.4'1'097   C92-098186-3

CONTENTS

FOREWORD

"There is no sound except of geese and the south wind in the maples, the coming of another spring." These closing words from Al Hochbaum's *The Canvasback on a Prairie Marsh* convey the spirit that he saw and felt in nature and so ably passed on to others. Al Hochbaum was a master interpreter of wildlife and wild places. When he died on March 2, 1988 he left behind the outstanding literary and artistic record of a remarkably curious and perceptive mind. Privileged were those who knew this quiet-spoken and committed "man of the marsh."

Al Hochbaum was born and educated in the United States; his Canadian journey had its roots in the drought of the 1930s that played havoc with duck numbers on the prairies of western Canada. Growing concern for these captivating birds brought together two men who greatly influenced Al's life— James Ford Bell, U.S. sportsman and operator of a wild duck hatchery on Manitoba's Delta Marsh and Aldo Leopold, a leader in the fledgling field of scientific wildlife management. These men saw in Al's talent and dedication the prospect for expanding the existing hatchery facilities at Delta, into a center for unlocking the secrets of duck biology and abundance.

One can easily imagine the early discussions that took place at the University of Wisconsin between Professor Leopold and Al Hochbaum, one of the professor's graduate students. Leopold would have described Bell's idea for a research station as a noble endeavor but one marked by unpredictable results and an uncertain future. The student no doubt questioned the wisdom of pursuing his career at Delta, a remote commercial fishing and summer cottage village lying on a beach ridge separating Lake Manitoba from the vast Delta Marsh. To the everlasting benefit of waterfowl lovers, student Hochbaum packed his bags and the rest is history.

His task was to bring the vision of a duck research station at Delta to life. It was a huge challenge. Fortunately Al had the presence and invaluable cooperation of three Delta residents: Bell's hatchery superintendent Ed Ward, who had a wealth of local knowledge and experience, Ed's daughter Joan, Al's "Lady of the Marsh," and Ed's son Peter, a talented wildlife interpreter and accomplished artist in his own right and station manager during Al's period as director.

At the outset no one could predict that the center would become such a successful venture and contribute so greatly to modern waterfowl management. The station was a private undertaking. It was not affiliated with any government or university. To become recognized the station needed to produce scholarly research that was accepted by the broader community of scientists. The station began producing research papers almost immediately. Then in 1944 Al's award-winning book, *The Canvasback on a Prairie Marsh*, brought the Delta Waterfowl Research Station into prominence.

In a short time "Delta" was considered the preeminent institution concerned with unraveling the mysteries of ducks in their breeding grounds. Not surprisingly, the station became a mecca for waterfowl biologists and allied scientists, while universities identified it as a superior location for graduate student research. During Al's tenure as director of the station, seventy-seven graduate students from thirty-four universities carried out research there. The University of Manitoba recognized Al's achievements at Delta by awarding him an Honorary Doctor of Laws degree in 1962.

Al gave credit for the station's growth to the opportunities and guidance provided by the Board of Trustees to whom Mr. Bell had turned over the reins of the station. The board consisted of conservation-minded individuals from many walks of private life in Canada and the United States who met at Delta for a few days each summer. Their simply stated objective, which coincided with that of the station's founder, was "doing something for the birds." Under Al's leadership this goal was attained with great distinction.

Although Al's first commitment was to the advancement of knowledge about waterfowl through basic research, he was extremely concerned about the everyday plight of ducks. Land- and water-use proposals that he believed would impact on ducks in his beloved province rarely escaped his written or spoken word. In recognition of the valuable role he played as an early and respected wildlife conservationist in Canada, he was appointed a member of the prestigious Order of Canada in 1978.

The duck fraternity remembers Al as the foremost champion of the bird in the hunting-versus-habitat controversy. He believed that excessive harvest had created a surplus of breeding habitat while others argued that the habitat had become so degraded that it could no longer attract and sustain breeding duck populations as it had in earlier times. Al's remedy was to significantly reduce the harvest; the counter remedy was to enhance the habitat. This difference of opinion created a quandary for waterfowl managers since both sides could produce evidence to support their respective positions. The debate, which went public and is ongoing, was valuable in that it forced governments to face both sides of the issue and to strive for a carefully balanced overall waterfowl management program.

Al Hochbaum never retired in the usual sense of the word; he went from Director of the Delta Waterfowl Research Station to its Writer-in-Residence, to free-lance writer and artist. In the latter capacity he turned his many and varied talents toward other loves in his life: Canada's northland, timber wolves, and caribou. His work in these areas, although lesser known and partly unfinished, maintained the high standards he set for waterfowl and marsh studies.

Al was honored many times for his professional accomplishments. Combining crystal-clear writing with superb artwork. His major books (*The Canvasback on a Prairie Marsh*, 1944; *Travels and Traditions of Waterfowl*, 1955; *To Ride the Wind*, 1973) received literary awards and are classics in natural history literature. But the recognition that probably brought him the greatest personal satisfaction was receipt of the 1980 Aldo Leopold Memorial Award from his peers "for distinguished service to wildlife conservation." This is the highest honor given by The Wildlife Society and it is named in memory of Aldo Leopold, Al's mentor and a founder of the wildlife management profession.

Sir Peter Scott, world famous naturalist, author, and painter, once paid the following tribute to Al: "It takes a rare, and a brave, talent to find simple truths in the immensely complicated and unendingly fascinating natural world around us and, having found them, to proclaim their truth simply. That Al has done, with patience, persistence and great effect, for a full generation."

And, if I may add, for the pleasure and enlightenment of generations to come through his earlier published work and now by way of the essays in this new book.

Gene Bossenmaier
Mayview, Saskatchewan

INTRODUCTION

Hans Albert Hochbaum was my father. He was born in 1911 in Greeley, Colorado and spent his youth in the mountains of Idaho, yet very early in life he gave his allegiance to the prairies. He loved grassland and marshes and the creatures that make the wilderness their home. His father had taught him to respect nature and from the age of three when he marveled that ducks always knew their way home he was curious to know how nature worked.

My father's academic career began at Cornell University studying agriculture, as his father wished. But George Sutton, one of his professors, persuaded him to expand his interest areas to include science, art, and ornithology. After that birds occupied most of his time. He observed them, studied them, and painted them. Waterfowl, especially ducks, became his special interest and he was concerned for their future. From the beginning he recognized that if we didn't take care of our birds many of them would become extinct. He set out to protect what the birds require for life, recognizing the importance of a holistic approach to environmental management that included the activities of man as a dominating force.

When my father was a new graduate, consideration of the environment was not a familiar topic. He learned much from the work of Charles Elton who used such new words as "ecology" to link organisms and their surroundings. Then he read Aldo Leopold's 1933 publication, *Game Management,* and headed for Wisconsin to learn first-hand about Leopold's work. My father became an extra family member in the Leopold household and the two men roamed the woods together observing and talking and formulating their theories about wildlife preservation and the protection of game. At that time my father studied wildlife management at the University of Wisconsin and when he graduated Leopold wanted him to become involved with woodlots and small game management, but circumstances influenced him in another direction. In 1938 he accompanied Leopold and Miles Pirnie on a trip to Delta Duck Station and its hatchery in Manitoba, Canada. Here he lost his heart forever to the marsh and the hatchery manager's daughter, Joan Ward, whom he married the following year.

The hatchery fascinated my father. It had been constructed by General Mills magnate James Ford Bell on land he owned on the marsh. It was his intention to raise two ducks to be released to the wild to replace every duck that was shot during the fall hunting season at Delta. At that time the marsh teemed with more than 400,000 mallards, redheads, green-winged teals, and canvasbacks and my father foresaw a great opportunity for research. He wanted to stay. The research my father did over the next two years was the basis of his Master of Science thesis which was published in book form in 1944— *The Canvasback on a Prairie Marsh.* It is still a classic in ornithology. The scientific knowledge that was gained at Delta through the years forms the basis of today's waterfowl and wetlands management practices.

My father believed that ducks are adaptable creatures that enjoy a long natural life, have high reproduction potential, and can adjust to changes in landscape, climate, and the activities of man. He wanted to keep the birds with us and his conservation philosophy was basically very simple—protect local ducks until the young and brood hens are well on the wing. I heard him say this hundreds of times. He also believed that farmers should be reimbursed to encourage them to provide nesting grounds for ducks since studies revealed that most ducks are hatched on privately owned farm lands. The continuing decline of ducks during the forties, fifties, and sixties was of great concern to my father. He foresaw a growing scarcity of ducks on the prairies and this has now come about. Today the decline is so serious that the future of ducks is uncertain.

Research and observation were vital to the formulation of my father's ideas about birds. He spent thousands of hours tramping the marsh watching bird behavior. He was one of the first to learn about the territorial behavior of birds; their courting, breeding, and migration instincts; and the aggression they display under some conditions. My grandmother told me that when my father was a young man, he became so engrossed in his observations and theories of birds that he extended his wanderings in the woods and often forgot to come home. He was oblivious to time and she actually tied a string on his finger to remind him that meals and a bed were waiting. I don't think he ever changed. Observing, recording, developing new theories, sketching, and painting made him happy all his life. The work he did at Delta on waterfowl habits and migration earned him an Honorary LL.D. This work was later published as *Travels and Traditions of Waterfowl.*

My father loved ducks, and what he learned about their behavior helped him to understand man and formulate his own philosophy of life. He said that the greatest unspoiled wilderness was probably the search for Truth and the one who seeks this wilderness will find the trail just as untraveled as that behind a white-footed mouse or a desert bighorn.

My father was ahead of his time. He recognized the need for conservation as he acknowledged man's shortcomings in the role of partner with the environment. But he never despaired because he accepted the human condition and thought that man wanted to and would gradually learn to use the land well. His thinking greatly influenced Leopold's most well known writing, "Thinking Like a Mountain," which is one of ecology's clearest parables about consequences of human behavior.

Before my father retired in 1970, Delta had published more rescearch papers on duck behavior and ecology than the Canadian and American presses combined. I have selected several of his essays and sketches mostly done between 1939 and 1948, although one encompasses 1982, that show the range of his thoughts and interests. They articulate notions and ideas that became known in the next thirty years in the writings of such wildlife scientists as Tinbergen, Lorenz, Morse, Klopfer, and Ardrey.

My father's knowledge was far-reaching and his insights about wildlife and man were profound. His conclusions seem fresh and appropriate, even today.

1 MY PRAIRIE HOME

O prairie mother, I am one of your boys.

CARL SANDBERG

My home is the prairie. Mine is a land where the sky comes down all around and the hills are far, far beyond: where a man's head is always high and he may see to the end of the earth. Here life is met each dawn at eye level. Here day ends with a majesty of light and color the hill people can never know. This is a country of a thousand ballads, but the best songs are sung by prairie chicken with the first soft winds of spring, by meadowlarks when fields are green with wheat and barley, or by wild geese honking their farewells in October. The prairie is the playground for the north wind running free from the Arctic without halt, and for the blizzarding snow that cuts like sand, dumping drifts behind every willow clump, and banking reservoirs for April water over sloughs and potholes, lakes and marshes, so that when spring comes again the sky will be laced with the wildfowl that make this wide country their home.

The great heartland of North America is prairie. It stretches from the bur-oaks of Bowling Green in Ohio, west to the Rocky Mountains, and crosses these by way of passes to the Great Basin country beyond the Continental Divide. Prairie reaches from the short-grass plains in the southern states north to the wooded edge of the Precambrian Shield in Canada. When the French adventurers, who first penetrated these wilds, found immense grass-covered plains in the center of the forests, J. Fenimore Cooper wrote in his introduction to *The Prairie*,[1] they naturally gave them the name "prairie" which was their word for grasslands. As the English succeeded the French and found that this peculiarity of nature was unlike anything they knew, and for which they had no English name, they continued to use the French name to distinguish these natural meadows. In this manner the word "prairie" was adopted into the English tongue.

In his book, Cooper acknowledged two kinds of prairie. East of the Mississippi the treeless openings were comparatively small, fertile, and always surrounded by forest. West of the Mississippi, however, the great prairie resembled the steppes of Tartary. Both were notable, Cooper said, for their scarcity of wood and were considered incapable of sustaining a dense human population.

Today's maps reflect these differences. As the country has grown, the prairie towns of the rich Middle West are often in sight of one another; but the map for much of the land west of the 100th meridian is thinly spotted with names. Often there are many miles between neighboring ranch houses, and the vast ranges are nearly as vacant of human habitation to this day as when Owen Wister's Virginian rode that way.

The prairies of Indiana, Illinois, and Wisconsin were long grasses, sometimes tall enough to hide the cattle that early settlers brought to that lush country, and always so high as to polish the horseman's stirrups. The long-grass prairie is now technically known as true prairie. It reaches west of the Mississippi for about one hundred miles, more or less, in the United States, its margin bending northwest to parallel the edge of the Aspen Parkland in Manitoba and Saskatchewan in Canada. Beyond, westward, grasses were shorter; indeed, on the western plains the ground cover did not hide the hocks of buffalo. This was short-grass prairie, now called mixed prairie. There has never been a sharp division between these two grasslands. Between the Red River of the North and the 100th meridian in North Dakota and Canada there is a transition zone where the dominance of true prairie depends upon the shape of the land and the exposure to the elements of earth and climate. The long grasses thrive on darker soils and heavier moister situations.

After the French, in 1803, sold their rights to much of this vast meadow and plain, there came about a slow but steady agricultural conquest. In the United States the pioneers emerged from the timber to reach the prairie between 1803 and 1840. In Canada, arriving by way of Hudson Bay and the Nelson River Valley in 1820, their presence confirmed by the Treaty of Ashburton, the settlers established western Canada as far south as the 49th parallel. The earliest newcomers built their homes where woods and grasses met, for prairie life seemed to have many disadvantages, not the least of which were the impassable snowdrifts and mud holes in late winter and spring, the furious wind coming without barrier out of the northwest, and the lack of wood for fuel.

pp16-7   Cattail marsh near Basswood, Manitoba. *Kodachrome 64. f4.5 @ 125 sec. 35mm elmarit lens, Leica R4 camera.*

On prairie trails in Manitoba, poles and stakes were set out to guide winter travelers, but long before thaw these stakes had vanished as those who passed by picked them up for firewood.

It was not until about 1850 that the pressure of increasing populations encouraged the settlement of the wide lands in Indiana and Illinois, urging movement still farther westward to regions even more barren of trees. Wherever the pioneers spied a clump of elm or a grove of bur-oak, there they settled, eventually to dot the maps with tree-named towns, the Elm Creeks of Manitoba and Nebraska, Maple Plains of Minnesota and Maple Creeks of Saskatchewan, the Oaklands and Oakvilles, the Willow Bends and Poplar Bluffs. The first to arrive set up their homes under shade and in lee of the wind, built the first church, and left those who followed to spread out over the barren countryside or to press still farther west.

As agriculture became established, it was soon clear that the long-grass prairie need not always be treeless. Homesteaders planted groves of green ash, cottonwood, and box elder to shield their buildings; and where they settled within a day's travel of woodland, they excursioned for spruce seedlings to plant before the house—one on the right, one on the left. As the plantings thrived, the clean sweep of horizon became broken by low, blunt-edged blocks of woods, which from a distance had the appearance of steep banks or jutting headlands. These became known prairie-wide as bluffs.

However, it was more than planted bluffs that grew. At first, as the Indians fired the prairies year after year, the annual planting did not take hold, being forever set back by the spring flames. When the Indian departed or changed his ways, and the free run of fire was stopped by roadways and plowed fields, grass no longer could hold its dominance as climax cover. Poplar and willow, maple, ash, and oak took foothold on untilled land and the farmer soon was obliged to take axe in hand when he sought to claim more acreage.

As settlers came farther west into the land of mixed prairie, the Indians departed or retreated behind reservation boundaries; yet trees did not take hold. They grew only where they had been in the beginning, along watercourses or in coulees where lingering snowdrifts allowed moisture enough for woody growth and where there was protection from the relentless wind and grass fires. The settlers could not always establish trees about their buildings, and to this day many farmsteads and ranches in Saskatchewan and the western Dakotas are naked, while villages are shaded only where there is water to spare.

The open ranges of the West have been settled almost to their capacity. Cattle replace the buffalo, and the howl of the wolf lives in the memories of only the oldest inhabitants. Over much of the prairie range, east and west, the original flora has gone from all but the smallest nooks and corners of unused land and the buffalo is not the only member of the fauna lost forever.

The North American prairie is now as tame as it is rich, tame overall except for the countless numbers of prairie marshes still remaining, many as wild and pristine with the coming of spring as in the days of the pioneers. Marshes large and small are as typical of the northern and central prairies as were the grasses themselves. Meltwater lingers in broad, reedy shallows from April onwards; long winding sloughs remain wet and marshy after the spring runoff has swept through the sluggish drainage courses, and on the slopes there are tens of thousands of round little bulrush-edged potholes, wet except in the driest years. In Manitoba, Saskatchewan, and the Dakotas there are settled districts that hold one hundred and twenty-five or more small marshes per section of farmland, with as many as one hundred pairs of breeding ducks for every square mile, except during years of drought. The traveler crossing this tame country meets the handiwork of man on every side; but when day ends and the foreground darkens against the afterglow, the glare of sunset is mirrored by innumerable pockets of reed and water. Wheat and barley or overgrazed pastureland are forgotten against the flame of prairie sky, and the view is the same as met the eye of the first pioneer and quite the same, indeed, as the native Indian knew it since all time before. Wildfowl, dark against the glow,

are constantly in sight—darts of canvasback or redhead in erratic flight, several drakes in chase after a single hen. Again and again a mallard or northern pintail or gadwall male rises in swift, deliberate territorial pursuit after a not-yet-settled pair. Reflections on the water are rippled by the activities of courting or feeding birds.

This is the land of marshes. Here on the prairies of Canada and the United States are the most beautiful, the most productive marshlands in all the world, each a heritage of wilderness in a region of North America that has been almost completely domesticated in three or four generations of human settlement. Only the great-great-great grandfathers remember the buffalo and the passenger pigeons. Even so, children born in this decade may be witness to a local spectacle of wildfowl as massive as any that were first seen by the pioneers. Great numbers of ducks that have lingered with us into the 20th century have done so largely because of the abundance and productivity of prairie marshes.

The word "marsh" comes to us from the Latin *mariscus*, the Low German *Marsch*, the Anglo Saxon *mersc* or "wet ground," and *mere* or "lake." Marish was used in 18th century England but is now obsolete. Webster defines "marsh" as a "tract of low land, usually or occasionally covered with water, or very wet and miry, overgrown with coarse grasses or with clumps of sedge."[2] Yet the definition of the obsolete marish is more concise: "low ground, wet or covered with water and coarse grass." The lexicographers, taking a broad look at their subject, leave the reader to understand that water plus herbaceous growth together make a marsh and that "clumps of sedge" and "coarse grasses" are a short way of saying that about seventy families of plants make up the flora of North American marshes, with some families, such as pondweeds, represented by many species.

Among technicians there is not yet clear agreement as to what a marsh really is. G. Evelyn Hutchinson of Yale University, who has given us the classic treatise on how marshes were formed, does not even use the word "marsh" in his

Mallards/northern pintails, Quill Lake, Saskatchewan. Kodachrome 64. f2.8 @ 250 sec. 50mm summicron lens, Leica R4 camera.

discussion of their beginnings.[3] J. G. Needham and J.T. Lloyd, world-respected authorities on inland waters, define marsh as a "meadow-like area overgrown with herbaceous aquatic plants such as cattails, rushes, and sedges,"[4] while R. L. Smith described a marsh as "wetlands in which the dominant vegetation consists of reeds, sedges, grasses, and cattails; essentially they are wet prairies."[5] I suspect that a marsh is best defined as a lake in the process of degeneration. "The life span of all freshwater lakes is usually short in terms of geologic times," says James H. Zumberge in *The Lakes of Minnesota*;[6] and he points out that rigid definitions of lakes, ponds, and marshes would lead to much confusion, since what was originally considered a lake might be modified by natural processes within the course of a few years to a dry basin.

A marsh, then, is a span of shallow water where vegetation grows with its roots beneath the surface, only leaves and flowers emerging. Indeed, shallowness is fundamental, or else there could not be the emergent flora that makes a marsh different from other wet places. But the bottom may be soft or hard, the area large or small, and the water acid or alkaline.

Wherever there is a marsh, whatever its size, however domestic its surroundings, there you find a bit of wilderness, a gem carried over from times past to be enjoyed by present generations of human beings, a place which in our time is quite the same as when seen by the first man.

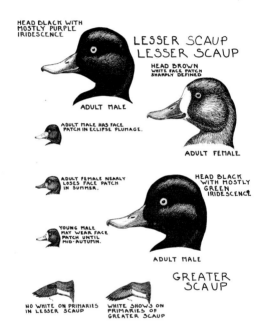

LESSER SCAUP
LESSER SCAUP

HEAD BLACK WITH
MOSTLY PURPLE
IRIDESCENCE

ADULT MALE

HEAD BROWN
WHITE FACE PATCH
SHARPLY DEFINED

ADULT MALE HAS FACE
PATCH IN ECLIPSE PLUMAGE.

ADULT FEMALE

ADULT FEMALE NEARLY
LOSES FACE PATCH
IN SUMMER.

HEAD BLACK
WITH MOSTLY
GREEN
IRIDESCENCE

YOUNG MALE
MAY WEAR FACE
PATCH UNTIL
MID-AUTUMN.

ADULT MALE

GREATER
SCAUP

NO WHITE ON PRIMARIES
IN LESSER SCAUP

WHITE SHOWS ON
PRIMARIES OF
GREATER SCAUP

*right   Aerial potholes,
Minnedosa, Manitoba.
Kodachrome 64. f5.6 @
500 sec. 28mm elmarit lens,
Leica R4 camera.*

The study of ducks has been my lifelong occupation and it is my experience that ducks and marshes and agriculture are interrelated. Since 1947 Canadian and American biologists have conducted annual surveys and studies of the duck nesting grounds of North America. The results of the studies reveal that most wild ducks are produced on the prairies, the black duck and wood duck being major exceptions. At least 98 percent of this prairie duck production is on private land, mostly farmland. This major product of wildfowl is yielded every year at no cost to the government and no cost to the individual. Canvasback, redhead, mallard, northern pintail, and all other ducks are mostly a free contribution by farmers to the citizens of North America.

Why do ducks prefer farmland? There are tens of thousands of ponds and lakes in the spruce country east and north of Delta in Manitoba, but these are used by few nesting ducks because there is little food in nearly sterile waters. Ducks, like farmers, depend upon rich land during the stressful period of production. Good land supports rich slough and pothole marshes, alive with plant and animal foods mother ducks and their young require during spring, summer, and early fall. Look at a map of the prairie provinces. Where there are many towns there are also many farms. It is within this farming range that we find the finest duck nesting country in the world.

Nearly every farm on the prairies has the capacity to produce ducks, although not all farmland is equally productive. Some of the best is in the pothole country west of Neepawa or south around Baldur in Manitoba. Back in the 1940s an award-winning study of renesting was carried out for ducks.[7] Most of the work, based on the study of several hundred ducks' nests, was conducted on farmland, hay meadow, and pasture on the road between Delta and Oakland. It was found that female ducks return in spring to nest in the same fields where they nested the previous year. Many hens came back to nest within a short distance—sometimes only a few feet—from the previous year's nest. When a

northern pintail or a northern shoveler nest was destroyed by skunk or crow, the study found that the mother duck nested again. Some nested a third time after their second nest was destroyed. These prairie ducks are persistent in their drive to hatch a new generation!

Another study of duck nesting[8] was carried out on twenty-five square miles of farmland south of Delta Marsh. This work depended not only on close cooperation with farmers but also on their help and advice. There were twelve duck nests per square mile on this intensely cultivated range. Of course, back in the 1940s and 50s you didn't need to make a study to realize the presence of nesting ducks. Driving from Delta to Portage la Prairie on the Town Line any day in spring you were seldom out of sight of pairs or lone drakes of mallard, pintail, and other species.

Back in the 1930s duck production on farmland was almost equally divided on both sides of the international boundary. As many ducks were produced in the prairie states of Wisconsin, Minnesota, Iowa, Nebraska, and the Dakotas as in the Canadian prairie provinces. But then, especially since 1946, there was massive drainage of farmland marshes in the United States. Whole counties became virtually duckless during the nesting season. Current estimates (*ed. note:* still true in 1994) hold that 75 to 85 percent of prairie ducks are now produced in Canada. This imbalance does not mean a Canadian increase; it is a measure of the decline in the United States. Stateside farmers decided to raise fewer ducks and more domestic crops.

An underlying philosophy has emerged from this. Farmers, duck hunters, almost anyone south of the line, believe that this serious problem has a ready-made solution. They say, "Well sure, we are producing fewer ducks down here

right Northern shoveler, Minnedosa, Manitoba. *Kodachrome 64. f4 @ 250 sec. 180mm apo-telyt-r lens, Leica R4 camera.*

far right Northern pintails in flight, Big Grass Marsh, Manitoba. *Kodachrome 64. f4 @ 250 sec. 90mm summicron lens, Leica R4 camera.*

26

but, after all, most come from Canada and we (meaning the United States) are sending millions of dollars to Canadians every year. It is a matter of history that back in the 1950s a bill was proposed to build marshes to help offset losses of marshland from drainage in the States." What they say is true, but this is not the answer to the decline in duck production.

Most ducks flying over Canada and the United States are a product of Canadian farmlands. If they are lucky the ducklings hatch in the spring and grow their flying feathers and gain strength during the hot summer. Then comes frost and ducks depart southward. As they travel, our prairie farm ducks are looking for a haven in the south that will offer protection until they head northward once again. By the time they are ready to return to Canada many ducks are paired or engaged in the delicate rituals of courtship. This is a critical time for ducks and it is important that the reproduction cycle is allowed to proceed.

If too many adult ducks are lost at this time, not enough of them are returned to Canada in spring to make use of the many fine marshes still remaining in Manitoba. Even in recent dry years, there were many good sloughs and nesting places with few or no nesting ducks to use them. As the years pass, as far as ducks are concerned, Canadians are in the position of

the farmer who faces spring without enough seed or the rancher who lacks cattle for his rich pasture. The nesting pairs are our capital stock, so to speak: and when this capital stock is gone, it is difficult to replace. Years ago an old wildfowler exclaimed, "You can't make ducks with dollar bills." Ducks are hardly different from farm produce: it takes wheat to make more wheat, cattle to make more beef, and ducks to make more ducks.

From the publicity Delta Waterfowl Research Station has received it is easy for some to believe that the decline of ducks has been confined to this area. Delta Marsh, as it is called, has always been a good producer of ducks. Yet in the overall picture, we must place it in perspective. Delta is fifty square miles of nesting range. The Minnedosa pothole country is four thousand square miles of duck nesting country, much of it, even in Delta's best years, more productive than Delta Marsh. Moreover, duck nesting on the Portage plains reaches far out beyond the big Marsh. Delta's major function, and it is a vitally important one, is as a spring and autumn gathering place for all species, and as a molting area for mallard, pintail, and other dabbling ducks. Only a fraction of the ducks seen at Delta in autumn are a product of this Marsh. The majority come from far and wide over the prairies. The decline of summer and autumn birds so noticeable at Delta reflects a prairie-wide decline—a massive reduction of birds that once congregated here from distant nesting grounds. In the middle 1950s there were one hundred thousand to four hundred thousand mallards using the Delta Marsh during August through October. Their twice-daily flights to and from the grain fields made a spectacle as imposing, perhaps, as the flights of the passenger pigeon.

However, with the massive reduction in mallards and pintails, the farmers' problem of ducks feeding off their land virtually ended. Adult birds, which are our capital stock, are gone. Now there are not enough breeders to use the enriched wetlands. The birds have not recovered. (*ed. note:* A current waterfowl

management plan seeks to restore duck numbers.) In 1981, the Delta Marsh peak for mallards was less that twenty-four thousand, this estimate based on an actual count of only three thousand birds. The food is still there for these transients. In 1981 and 1982, the crop of sago pondweed and other marsh foods was excellent over most of the marsh. The roosting places are still there at the south end of Cadham Bay along Portage Creek, and along the shores of Lake Manitoba which remain a virtual sanctuary. The farm fields are still loaded with wheat and barley, with corn now an added enticement. So we ask ourselves, "How will the dollars invested in dams, dikes, and pumps to make marshes bring about the recovery of the hundreds of thousands of mallards that came here every fall to feed on our grain fields?"

In the 1950s, farmers, the Manitoba government, and private conservation groups worked hand-in-hand to control duck depredations and reduce losses. Refined scaring techniques, feeding stations, and lure crops were part of the solution. I am confident that if there should be a recovery of ducks on the prairies and in the Delta Marsh, any other problems caused to the farmer by field feeding will be handled in a satisfactory manner. But, first let us bring back the ducks.

It was April on the big meadow. Snow no longer covered the brown dead grass of the open marsh, although a few tiny drifts clung solidly beneath the stunted bur-oaks in the prairie grove. Winter held only a weak claim to the meadow. Each night thin new ice formed on the open water but it was gone by noon. In the big bay the pack ice honeycombed and fell apart. A few ducks rested on the small patch of open water at the edge of the marsh and more appeared in the sky.

From the south, two northern pintail, drake and hen, matched wing beats in rhythmic flight. Drawing their slim bodies swiftly forward, they circled and dipped over the broad meadow and the icy bays and sloughs. The long lines of the drake paralleled the prairie; but unlike the tousled meadow, his feathers were in tight and orderly formation. There was no white whiter than his breast. Wedging into the brown of his handsome head, the white met the black of his long tail far back under his sleek body. Each feather, patterned like a fine engraving, overlapped the next from his shining head to the five-inch pin or central tail feather. Outstretched he must have spanned a full twenty-nine inches from the tip of his grey bill to the tip of his tail; wing-tip to wing-tip, thirty-seven. His weight now, at the end of his long flight north, would be less than two pounds.

above Northern pintail pair in flight, Delta, Manitoba. *Kodachrome 64. f5.6 @ 500 sec. 180mm apo-telyt-r lens, Leica R4 camera.*

left Northern pintail pair, Brandon, Manitoba. *Kodachrome 64. f5.6 @ 250 sec. 180mm apo-telyt-r lens, Leica R4 camera.*

The hen he followed was small and drab greyish-brown with a freckled grey bill. Smaller than the drake by a full half-pound, she measured about twenty-one inches in length and twenty-nine across her wings. These wings, which should have had ten large feathers each were not the same; the left showed a wide and vacant notch. Lost to a hunter over Sioux Pass last October I suspected. Only two short stubs remained where round blunt lead had cut out two hollow quills. Yet minus the two primaries, she still flew straight and fast. Her wings had taken her many thousands of miles the past year.

33

From this very meadow last August she had taken off for the sloughs and corn stubbles of Iowa, then to the lakes and reservoirs of Texas, on to the lagoons of Mexico, and now, six months later, she had returned again to the meadows and marshes of Manitoba.

She was home. Home was the same few acres where the previous year's brood paddled its eight-veined wake behind her. Home was where the bone and down of two grey ducklings still bleached on a log near the den of a big brown mink. Man, the master of marsh and meadow, does not know how she is able to return to these same few acres again and again, but to the hen this spot is favored and familiar.

Dropping low, the pair circled. Their shadows caressed a hay stack capped with snowy-owl pellets. The ducks skimmed the old deer trail and climbed and crossed yellow reeds on the bay edge of newly opened water. Somewhere in this meadow, not too far from the bay, would be the nest site. Sometime within the week the site would be chosen. Already the urge to nest was great. For these two birds, the long migration flight had ended.

Early the next morning the pair cruised the meadow in searching flight, the hen still leading and her drake close beside her. Around once, then twice, and back again. With the site now chosen, the hen dropped obliquely down as her drake continued to circle, calling softly. Each whistle-call paused his flight as his grey bill opened, his brown head pulled back, and his long white neck arched handsomely. Four great circles were completed before he left her and glided off to a roadside ditch.

Alone now, the hen stood alert in the flat dead grass and looked around. Crisp, new ice broke beneath her toes. Into the air again and fluttering low she hovered over a pile of dead flax stems and dropped down at its edge in a grassy clump. Here she rested and explored the weathered stems beneath her feet.

By mid-morning the sun had risen into the blue sky. The hen stood and stretched her wings and tucked a few grasses around her one slender green egg. Here it was to lie in the thin shadow of dried thatchgrass leaves, the life within it at the mercy of crow, gopher, skunk, and spring's freak cold or flood. Leaving now, the hen flew away to a shallow slough.

She was light and graceful as she came into view of the waiting drake. He rose to meet her. Synchronizing their flight, she and her good-looking mate disappeared over the big marsh. Each morning the pair came to the meadow. Each day the drake waited nearby at the water's edge and each day he was joined by his hen and together they disappeared over the big marsh. For eight days the pair continued to arrive, but on the ninth day they did not come.

Her mate had abandoned her and was wandering the marsh with other bachelor drakes. As the attentions from her drake grew fewer, the hen's attachment for her eggs increased, and she spent most of her day sitting on them. Beneath the concealing canopy of grasses, beneath her grey breast, were eight green eggs. Around them lay a deep band of belly down, plucked from her own soft breast. It was with this that she blanketed them when she made her daily trip to feed.

Day after day she sat beneath this canopy. The nights had grown shorter, now only briefly punctuating the long span of sunlight. Two weeks had passed. She had spent over three hundred hours on the nest. Once each day she left the eggs to feed in the nearby prairie pond.

The canopy had grown green and the grasses waved with each gust of the prairie breeze. In the farmer's fallow field yellow mustard threatened to spread its noxious seeds.

Northern pintail hen on nest, Delta, Manitoba. *Kodachrome 64. f8 @ 250 sec. 135mm elmarit lens, Leica R4 camera.*

It was from that field that the threat came—a red monster coughing up and down the meadow's edge. Nearer and nearer the huge tractor moved, blackening the field behind its track. Unable to tolerate its approach, the hen fluttered, limp-winged, across the plowed land. Biting sharply into the soft earth, a big rubber tread seized a lump of grey belly-down from the nest. Round and round it went, down the stretch of field. Eight green eggs rode over the shining plowshare and were engulfed in a narrow grave. Along with the yellow blooms of mustard they were buried beneath the black monotony of the rich prairie earth.

After feeding in the nearby flooded field the hen returned. Nothing was the same. Where were the green clumps of grasses, the waving yellow mustard, the friendly and familiar? Where were the long evening shadows cast by the tall giant mustard? For a week the hen loitered in the flooded field and fattened on the floating seeds and insects.

One quiet mid-morning two handsome drake pintails held their long necks high above the flooded grass a few yards from where she fed. Scattered round the shallow edges were a half-dozen more. She paused, raised her head, and eyed the drakes. Their plumage was bright and their tails were long. They looked just as her first drake had looked six weeks ago. Throwing her head back along her side she uttered a teasing "yank-yank-yank." Across the water sheet it went. Eight drake pintails held heads high. Like the reaction of young men to the flirtatious drop of a kerchief in a city park, the response of the drakes was electric.

All drake northern pintails, eight of them, moved toward her. Fluttering straight up she uttered another coaxing "yank-yank-yank" in mid-air and dropped again into the grass, the drakes following in pursuit. Up and up they went. With each teasing call her head went back. With each throw of the head her flight paused and she dropped momentarily, only to tower again, even higher and farther. All the drakes followed and were joined by others.

This was the towering flight of courtship, common among many ducks, but perfected only by the pintail. At a thousand feet above the meadow only two drakes remained. Another soaring thrust and all but one of these dropped out. Alone with her new mate she disappeared over the marsh.

Even in spring the chill morning dew hung on the meadow grasses. Yet the dawning hours buzzed with life as the ducks began moving. Over fields of glossy green wheat came a small flock of drakes. They had eaten waste barley on the prairie that morning and had now returned to rest in the big marsh. This was a bachelor band who had left their spring mates. Among them was the first great drake, now dull and bespeckled.

left   Northern pintail courtship flight, Delta, Manitoba. *Kodachrome 64. f5.6 @ 500 sec. 280mm apo-telyt-r lens, Leica R4 camera.*

His tail was blunt, for the long graceful central feather or pin was gone.

The sky was empty for only a moment. Then over the marsh two moving dots appeared: a pair of pintails, drake and hen, circling the meadow. This drake wore his courting coat white breast, brown head, and five-inch pin. The hen lacked two large feathers in her left wing.

As the drake circled back to the big marsh, the hen dropped down and stood near a black furrow, mirrored with June rain. Just one hundred twenty-five yards from a once familiar dry-grass canopy, a new nest was started and when completed held seven eggs. The lush green thatchgrass waved a blooming top and evidenced spring water standing there, for thatchgrass seldom blooms if in spring its feet are dry. This time there was hardly enough down to protect the eggs, but summer was friendly and no freak frost chilled the tiny young embryos within their green shells.

The day had been warm. Short-grass clumps made long blue shadows on the prairie flat and the hen loitered on the pothole rim eating water shrimps and floating seeds. Carefully she combed her feathers, arranging each one. Fat from her preen gland clung to her grey bill and coated each of her long wing shafts.

Pilfered northern pintail nest in stubble, Minnedosa, Manitoba. *Kodachrome 64. f8 @ 250 sec. 50mm summicron lens, Leica R4 camera.*

For six days she incubated her second set of eggs. Each afternoon or evening she fed alone on the pothole rim, oiled and arranged her feathers, and quietly returned to sit another twenty-four hours. Unhurried, she raised her head and took in the surrounding prairie. On the left slumbered a herd of cattle; on the right, some distance away, was her nest in the green thatchgrass. Fluttering into the air she circled the nest site but flared. A long running whistle made a dancing line in the still grass. A grey gopher dashed away. Cautiously now, the hen approached her eggs. Four had been broken. Egg smeared, the down lay scattered about the nest. The hen quickened her approach and moved swiftly to the nest. Carrying an eggshell in her bill, she flew off to the neighboring pothole, dropped it into the brown water, and circled back. Three such flights were made, three broken egg shells were removed. But the gopher's retreat from the nest was temporary. Each time the hen was away he returned to the nest and continued to pilfer, until at last no eggs remained. The hen rested, motionless, on the pothole edge. This time she did not circle back but flew away to the big marsh.

During the hot summer the July sun sucked abundant moisture from the prairie sloughs. Water weeds tangled in the shallow pond and small yellow buttercups struggled to hold their weak heads above water. Skimming for water spiders with their wide bills, a brood of six grey ducklings dispersed a fan of dancing circles around their mother.

Over one hundred days ago the hen had come to the meadow. So much had happened. The handsome drake, the first nest, the red tractor, the towering courtship with its teasing calls, the new mate, and the running whistle in the

Northern pintails jumping, Quill Lake, Saskatchewan. *Kodachrome 64. f5.6 @ 500 sec. 90mm summicron lens, Leica R4 camera.*

39

grass. Now, at last, from her third clutch of eggs she had brought off a brood of six. Late August found them in erratic flight, adult in size and feather, they circled aimlessly in wide and staggering loops and sky-tumbled the length of the long green slough.

Meanwhile, the hen retired to the marsh, and there she mingled with the growing flocks of "flappers" and awaited her winter plumage. For two weeks, while new flight feathers grew into place, she could not fly. Her old wing feathers were replaced too, and each wing now held ten strong shafts. How near, now, the great flight south, for as she molted, early migrants already streaked the sky. Yet, for her, alas, there was to be no flight.

October first was opening day of duck shooting. The pass between the bays was crowded with guns and hunters. Guns echoed along the wall of yellow reeds, and by mid-morning most ducks were flying high above gunshot, except for a small flock of birds newly arrived from the prairie fields. With full gullets they flew heavily and dropped fast to alight in the big marsh. Over the flashes of hot light they flared, and one that could not gain height glided down, carrying new lead. Into a small hidden pond she struggled, and there she fed on new seeds of pondweed and hid in the dense rim of rushes.

So it was that one November night, with little circles of ice growing on every bulrush spike, she was forced, inch by inch, toward the center of the shrinking pond. There, paddling helplessly to keep the small center open, she swam in a tiny circle, ever diminishing in its size, while the flight overhead grew thinner with the last straggling migrants going south. The wind had died, and soft snow-flakes hung in the sagging plumes of yellow cane. On the muskrat house the snow melted as it fell, but this warmth was waning also and at last, reluctantly, it yielded to the advancing white. A tiny drift formed around a frozen wing laid stiffly over new-formed ice around ruffled feathers of neck and head. Flake by flake it covered the body of the frozen bird. Winter had come to the meadow.

The brood is the family unit in the waterfowl society. It is made up of the young attended by the mother or by both parents. With geese and swans the male not only shares parental duties during the rearing period, but the family bond still holds as young parents move southward in the autumn. With the ruddy duck the drake frequently, but by no means always, remains with the hen as a member of the family; yet he departs from his parental role before the young are ready to fly, usually before the hen has abandoned her charges. With all the North American ducks the drake sometimes remains with hen and brood, but this is the exception rather than the rule. The mother duck takes the responsibility for the offspring. She guards the eggs and she cares for the young.

When a duckling first breaks from its shell it is capable of a complex set of actions. In the first twenty-four hours of life it can walk, swim, dive, bathe, preen, stretch, gape, and sleep with the same assurance as the adults. The preening actions of a tiny duckling are a wonder to behold. I watched a canvasback duckling less than a day

right   Female canvasback with young in nest, Minnedosa, Manitoba. *Kodachrome 64. f8 @ 250 sec. 90mm summicron lens, Leica R4 camera.*

below   Blue-winged teal duckling just hatched, Minnedosa, Manitoba. *Kodachrome 64. f6.3 @ 250 sec. 90mm summicron lens, Leica R4 camera.*

out of the shell. What attention it gave to the scapular tract, working the down with its bill, adjusting, straightening, billing, and then readjusting feathers that weren't even there. It preened its belly, then suddenly turned to give the final touch to the scapulars. Next the flank, the wings above and below, the rump, and the tail all received its attention. Indeed, there are few preening actions of the adult, the basic movements of which are not enacted by the duckling. When finally the plumage was in order, likely as not the downy would stretch up its neck, beat its diminutive wings, then just as the adult would do, the duckling stretched its neck downward, and held the bill agape, the duck's equivalent, I presume, of a yawn.

During the duckling's first forty-eight hours, feeding and drinking are accomplished. Actually, feeding movements begin shortly after hatching. I've noticed that when captive ducklings are drying off in the incubator trays you can hear the rattle of tiny bills as they experiment with the tray wire, straws, scraps of paper, or any small objects in the brooders. When food is placed before the infants on their second or third day it is billed, then eaten. Thus, at the beginning of life the duckling is ready to meet the world.

Of the objects that surround the infant when it enters the world, some evoke immediate reactions. The downy reacts to its brothers and sisters by associating with them, to its mother by following her, to water by swimming, diving, and bathing in it, and to small objects by billing them. It responds to a loud noise, my shout for instance, by "freezing" for a moment and ceasing its peepings. If I approach it rapidly it will run from me, although at this stage it is avoiding the large, moving object and not the enemy.

Canvasback brood, Minnedosa, Manitoba. Kodachrome 64. f8 @ 250 sec. 280mm apo-telyt-r lens, Leica R4 camera.

Within the first twenty-four hours wild young react to plant growth by seeking escape in it. This behavior, however, seems more highly developed in river ducks than in diving ducks, which when harassed, more frequently seek escape by moving to open water, then diving.

As the duckling grows older, other innate actions develop. When its wing feathers begin to grow the birds now and again are seen to sit back on the water and fan their wings. There is much evidence that such wing beating is not the process of learning to fly but is a matter of maturation of instinctive action; that is, the organ is ready before the instinctive coordination is there. But even in these preliminary movements the learning process is involved. For instance, when captive ducklings first fan their wings they face in any direction. Soon, however, they always face into the wind.

While flight itself is an innate action, the act of maneuvering the body through air successfully is learned through experience. On several occasions I have pursued fully grown young which, while racing across the water with wings beating, suddenly found themselves airborne in what I believe was their first flight. While the flight was successful, the movements did not seem as well coordinated as those of an adult. The young seemed to have particular difficulty in turning. Also the finer techniques of taking off and alighting are undoubtedly learned. Young pintails that I have watched taking wing for the first time left the water at a low angle, in contrast to the sharp upward rise of the adult pintail. This was likely due in part to the fact that the wing quills were still soft and blood-filled, and were unable to bear the strain of the more abrupt rise. Also the alighting movements are less expertly performed than those of the adult.

Close-up canvasback ducklings, Minnedosa, Manitoba. *Kodachrome 64. f6.3 @ 250 sec. 280mm apotelyt-r lens, Leica R4 camera.*

44

About the time the primary feathers begin to appear on the wing (the time varies according to species), the duckling's voice changes from that of the child to that of the adult. When a young mallard gives its first adult note the whole attitude of the bird is one of bewilderment and surprise. Twice I have seen this in the captive pens. The bird utters a rough, reedy "whank." Its companions are startled and quiet for a moment, and then the originator of the note looks around as if to say, "Who the dickens said that?" Researchers say[9] that when a duck performs an instinctive act for the first time, it generally shows surprise, hesitation, bewilderment, or even fear.

With the canvasback and redhead, actions similar to the neck-stretch courting posture of the adult appear early in life. In every instance where I have witnessed such behavior the young bird was startled, which was perhaps a fear reaction. Whether or not this movement is related to the similar action given in courtship I do not know. But in some other species the dominant courting actions are also the same as special actions given when danger threatens. The blue-winged teal's most conspicuous courting action is a rapid up and down bobbing of the head. The same action in adult and juvenile blue-winged teal (but not in downy young) is given immediately prior to flight when in autumn the bird is approached by a hunter.

Shortly after the young duck is flying it makes actions the same as those of courtship. I have seen juvenile canvasback, redhead, and American wigeon males going through all the courtship displays characteristic of the adult. Although the actions of such birds are performed more awkwardly than in the adult, I have also witnessed attempted copulation by ducklings and juveniles.

Some innate actions of ducklings are little used in later life. For example, all river ducks dive frequently for food as ducklings, but adult river ducks seldom dive beneath the surface except when harassed during the flightless period. At what stage the young forgo their diving I do not know. Once in late September I saw a band of fully grown juvenile blue-winged teal busily diving in five feet of water.

Early in life the duckling orients itself to its environment. In a banding trap I have frequently recaptured young birds time and time again, even though they are moved, as I have moved parentless young bluebills a quarter of a mile away from the trap after capture. I have made similar observations with young blue-winged teal and mallards. Again and again they quickly learned to orient themselves to the trap site, especially when my free meal of baited barley was there for the taking. I expect this particular ability has something to do with the hen's return each year to the area of the previous year's nest site.

above   Redhead drake diving to feed; canvasback drake in background, Basswood, Manitoba. *Kodachrome 64. f5.6 @ 500 sec. 180mm apo-telyt-r lens, Leica R4 camera.*

right   Blue-winged teal brood, Minnedosa, Manitoba. *Kodachrome 64. f8 @ 250 sec. 90mm summicron lens, Leica R4 camera.*

I knew by the way Archie slapped my mail down on the counter and by his inability to control the twitching at the corner of his mouth as he wrapped my bread that he had something important on his mind. I feigned disinterest, knowing that he would break the news, whatever it might be, before I left. When I was ready to leave I picked up my groceries and started for the door. It was then that Archie cleared his throat and said, with all the casualness that he could muster, "Seen any crows yet?"

I knew he was pleased with the startled look on my face as I dropped my packages and edged up to the counter again. "Damn it all Archie, you haven't beat me on the crows again this year!"

"Saw three this morning out by an ice pile."

Common crows feeding on white-tailed deer carcass. Jackson County, Missouri. Ektachrome 100. f11 @ 500 sec. 280mm apo-telyt-r lens, Leica R4 camera.

Archie was in a glow. Again he had made his main ornithological contribution of the year and he knew that for another season his name would top the list on my kitchen door. For those of the southland the crow is a common winter bird. But for us northerners their return in March is the most important sign of spring, and when they arrive we say goodbye to winter, although there may be weeks of icy weather for us to endure.

The crow is more than the herald of spring. In this country it is a sign of the times—a black mark evidencing man's conquest of the prairies just the same as fences, cultivated fields, and advertisements of soda pop. Although common now, the crow was just about as rare as fence lines when man first broke the prairie sod. The crow has come with and is evidence of the conquests of the plow.

Is the crow now friend or foe? Anyone who is a hunter, and anyone who is interested in bird life, is aware of the crow problem. And everyone who is aware takes sides. On one side is the sportsman group that is strong in its antagonism toward the crow and its proven depredations on the eggs of game birds. On the other side is the conservative group of non-hunting nature lovers who, admitting that crows eat duck eggs, contend nevertheless, that this is a part of the natural plan and that he who would reduce the number of crows is upsetting the beautiful plan of nature. There has been some friction and ill feeling between the two groups over this question.

For the conservatives let me say this. The natural plan was terribly upset long before anyone ever thought of the crow problem in this country. The crow is an alien here and not part of any plan. He is an intruder. Not only on the prairies but throughout much of Canada and the United States, the crow has extended its range and increased its numbers far beyond pristine populations, largely because of man's conquests of the land. The crow has followed agriculture to this country and has thrived. It has found abundant nesting places that did not exist on the original treeless prairie. It is not only present, but lives here in great numbers. Along the woodland borders of the Delta Marsh there is one crow's nest for every four acres. Where the crow lives beside the marshlands it preys

Editor's Note: The number of ducks and crows at Delta Marsh have diminished. In 1993 there were less than 5000 pairs of nesting ducks and about 10 pairs of nesting crows.

heavily on duck nests—not as a member of the original fauna, but as a highly successful invader. The crow is intelligent, high in the order of bird life, and well equipped to survive. It is firmly entrenched. What should we do about the crow's threat? In the face of a changing world we on the prairies should have the right to reduce the numbers of this species where we know its pressure is heavy on other species, such as ducks, in the highly concentrated nesting areas around marshlands.

The depredations caused by crows are obvious to anyone who gets out-of-doors in spring. Anyone who tramps the edge of the marshlands will find crow-eaten

Northern shoveler with brood in nest, Delta, Manitoba. *Kodachrome 64. f8 @ 250 sec. 135mm elmarit lens, Leica R4 camera.*

49

duck eggs under some willow or poplar. Studies by careful scientists have proven that in some regions crows prey very heavily on ducks.[10] The obvious conclusion is this: reduce the crows and we will have more ducks. True. But the danger in such thinking is that we and our administrative bodies may bring ourselves to believe that we can assure the success of ducks by killing crows. We may overrate the importance of the crow and in our enthusiasm, underrate the many other steps we might take towards the conservation of waterfowl. Many of the truths of nature are hidden and not readily apparent at first glance. The most beautiful truth is that, provided with natural marshland, ducks will reproduce their numbers successfully despite the presence of their natural predators. The ugly truth is that man has unnaturalized many of the marshlands. He allows cattle to overgraze their borders, he burns the marshland in April nesting time, and he takes off a hay crop before all the nesting is complete and hatching has occurred. Crows are only a small part of the picture. We cannot view crows, or any other predators, in isolation.

Upland nesting habitat, Quill Lake, Saskatchewan. *Kodachrome 64. f11 @ 250 sec. 50mm summicron lens, Leica R4 camera.*

50

The mallard duck is a successful species. It was in this world long before we arrived, and despite the many changes that man has effected on the earth, the mallard is still going strong. It is one of our wiliest, wariest game birds. I know of no other duck so continuously on the alert for the gunner, so quick to shy away from the hunter's carefully concealed blind, or so ready to flare out of gun-shot range. This striking greenhead seems to be equipped to carry on in spite of man's intervention.

The mallard is resourceful. It is able to survive under extremely adverse conditions and is capable of adapting itself to drastic changes in its environment. While many wild species have retreated before the advance of man, the mallard is still able to thrive. It is capable of surviving in the face of numerous enemies: it asks nothing of man except the right to follow its own natural way of life.

Is this true of all mallards? Certainly not. Long ago some of them made a bargain with man. "Here, you, don't be silly," man said. "You are nothing but a feathered fool to work so hard for your livelihood. If you will give up the rigorous ways of your wild natural life and come live under my care, you need not bother your head with another worry. I will supply you with the choicest foods and I will defend you from your natural enemies. I will house you in winter so that you won't even have to make the long, tiresome journey to the southland each autumn. I will protect your young and help you rear them. You will not have to work and you will want for nothing!" This was a good offer and many mallards fell for it. Some came into the fold of man, and the fat, potbellied ducks of our farmyards are their descendants.

This transition is still happening. Each year, many mallards cross the line from a free wild life to domesticity. You will see some of these in the ponds or lakes of our city parks. Many of them look like true wild mallards, but if you

left   Mallard pair, Lake Manitoba marshes. *Kodachrome 64. f4 @ 500 sec. 600mm/f-4 Nikkor super telephoto lens, Nikon F-4 camera.*

below   Mallard drakes, Lake Manitoba marshes. *Kodachrome 64. f4 @ 500 sec. 600mm/f-4 Nikkor super telephoto lens, Nikon F-3 camera.*

examine them carefully you will see that they are not the same. The tame park mallard is heavier set than his wild brother; his bill is shorter and he is slung low between his legs. He walks with more of a waddle and is less agile on his feet than the wild bird. More importantly, he has lost the migrating urge and remains at the park throughout the year. The female does not move to wild marshes to nest but lays her eggs and rears her young under the watchful eye of civilization. The park bird is not as active on the wing nor as graceful in movement as the wild bird. If the park bird were to be abandoned to the wilds it would be incapable of depending upon its own resources for survival. Its future depends upon its caretaker.

Are men like mallards? Probably the principles of survival are the same. Man's livelihood depends upon his ability to make his own way in his environment. Every man has to "scratch gravel" to survive in this world; his life and that of his family depend upon his resourcefulness. It is this, the necessity for each man to manage his own survival, that has made ours a strong vigorous nation. However, during the last twenty years, some men have put aside this independence. We are no longer like the pioneers. Hundreds of plans have been developed for making life easier for man by divesting him of the worries and trials of life. Social security has become man's caretaker.

Is this a good thing? As with the mallard a price must be paid. To trade any of the trials of natural survival for unnatural security means first the degeneration of the individual personality, followed by the degeneration of national self-esteem. A person who need not shoulder all the responsibilities for his future need not bother himself greatly about the present. In the presence of total economic security that is known in some parts of the world, the only real worry is not for the trials of living, but that the government providing that security might be replaced by some other government that would throw the people back to their heritage of individual resourcefulness. I think complete security would mean the end of democracy as we know it, because any people dependent upon the plans of their government for the plan of their individual

Mallard drake, full flight, Lake Manitoba marshes. *Kodachrome 64. f4 @ 500 sec. 600mm f-4 Nikkor super telephoto lens, Nikon F-4 camera.*

lives could no longer call themselves a democratic race. Just as the park mallard trades his right to the future for the questionable benefits of domesticity, so the people of a land abandon their right to a vigorous future by obliging themselves to their government for their easy security.

By its handouts, some governments promise a happier, more protected life for the people. Of course, happiness and security are wanted, but only if they are fashioned by the hands and minds of the people. The present and future, no matter how difficult they are, are the reponsibility of the people. If the government makes the way for us, then we have lost more than we could ever gain. We have the choice of two roads to follow, with no middle course. We can build ourselves into a strong, resourceful nation and like the wild mallard, stake our future on our ability, individually and nationally, to meet all the hardships of life and come out on top. Or we can follow the domestic mallard and accept a safe, although artificial, way of life in which the present may be pleasant enough, but the freedom is limited and the future uncertain.

left   Mallard drake, Lake Manitoba marshes. *Kodachrome 64. f4 @ 500 sec. 600mm f-4 Nikkor super telephoto lens, Nikon F-4 camera.*

below   Mallard pair, Delta, Manitoba. *Kodachrome 64. f4 @ 500 sec. 600mm f-4 Nikkor super telephoto lens, Nikon F-4 camera.*

Right   Mallards jumping from pothole, Lake Manitoba marshes. *Kodachrome 64. f4 @ 500 sec. 600mm f-4 Nikkor super telephoto lens, Nikon F-4 camera.*

7 DUCK PASSES

When in spring the transient ducks depart northward from Delta Marsh they cross the south shore of Lake Manitoba at special passes over which the first step into the North is made year after year. The flight to the passes is swift and direct; there is no hesitation, no circling. Nor is there conspicuous movement over the marsh during the day prior to their evening departures to suggest a preliminary reconnoitering of the terrain. Even in the dark the ducks select their route unerringly. My cottage is directly under a passageway. Some evenings when the northward flight continues long after twilight has faded, I hear the swishing sounds of their many bands overhead. Yet if I walk three hundred yards to the east, or cross the channel to the west, I am aware of no bird above me.

These lakeshore passes are the same for all species of ducks. In late April or early May when the main flights of redhead, canvasback, and lesser scaup thrust northward, they cross the wooded lake ridge at the same places that mallards and pintails used eight or ten days earlier. Some of the passes are old creek or channel beds, long dry and so obliterated by vegetation that they blend easily with the surrounding landscape. Several passes are open channels that still connect the marsh with Lake Manitoba. Others are at narrows where a marsh bay or a chain of sloughs edge close to the ridge, while the remainder show no formations of the past or present from which we may deduce the reasons for their use.

In general the span of a pass is a hundred to two hundred yards, although its core, through which the great body of birds moves, may be much narrower than this. This main line of flight over a pass may vary from day to day, the pathway within the boundaries apparently being dictated by the wind's direction.

It is not true that all traffic between marsh and lake follows these crossings. Watching the flights on a spring evening I have seen an occasional band traveling between passes. But so closely does the great majority hold to the aerial trails that the lanes are well known to all local residents, and their

Mallards in flight at sunset, Lake Manitoba marshes. *Kodachrome 64. f4 @ 500 sec. 600mm f-4 Nikkor super telephoto lens, Nikon F-4 camera.*

positions are clearly marked by the main lines of flight. The passes are located at convenient intervals along the lakeshore, averaging one or two per mile. But the ducks do not always select the nearest pass. Often they are seen to take off near one pass, only to fly some distance to make their crossing at another.

The use of the lakeshore passes is by no means confined to the spring flight. In fall, when the ducks pour out of the North, they are seen to enter the Marsh by way of the passes. In August and throughout the autumn, mallards that loaf on the lakeshore move over the passes in their twice-daily trips to the stubble fields. When a band is flushed in the Marsh the birds often move over the lake, but they do not cross the ridge by a direct route; they fly east or west, sometimes a considerable distance, to cross at a pass. One year a large band of pre-eclipse redhead drakes fed daily in a bay two miles east of Delta. Moving nightly to the lake, the drakes could have flown a quarter-mile due north for a direct route. Instead of taking this short-cut, however, they always flew west a mile to cross at a pass. I have watched the flights moving over the passes for only seven years, but the lanes have been the same for as many years as the oldest local resident can recall.

I doubt that ducks are guided over these crossings by an inborn heritage. The passes, I believe, are learned. With the Canada goose, which also follows special passageways over the lake shore, the heritage may be passed down from father to son, for the young accompany their parents in the southward journey from the breeding grounds. Presumably, through their association in travel with their parents, the young learn these steps in the migration highway. With ducks, on the other hand, the young do not travel with their parents after they have taken wing. Many people suspect that the duck learns the passes by two methods. First, conspicuous crossings, such as the open channels or the narrows, are probably learned through personal experience as a duck becomes familiar with its surroundings. Secondly, the less obvious lanes, such as the obliterated creek beds, are learned through the tradition that is carried in movement from one generation to another. Ducks are highly social animals and are greatly

pp62-3   Canada geese returning to lake after feeding in stubble, early evening, Lake Manitoba marshes. *Kodachrome 64. f4 @ 500 sec. 600mm f-4 Nikkor super telephoto lens, Nikon F-4 camera.*

influenced by the actions of companions. A duck flies where it sees other ducks flying.

Many of the drakes, following hens they met on the wintering grounds, have never taken the route before. Nor have many of the young birds. The tradition probably is carried from year to year by a small portion of the population. Tradition, of course, cannot account for the adherence to the migration route between the breeding marshes and the wintering waters; this may be followed through inborn guidance. The Delta lakeshore passes merely offer further evidence that the individual's course within the migration route is modified by personal experience, this being gained independently or by following the movements of companions already familiar with the terrain.

However these passes are learned and for whatever reasons, they are special crossing points for the ducks, and it is clear that these pinpoints on a map are steps in migration. There is no blind surge north or south. The movement is precise, and the small steps are the same from year to year. Is the entire migration route made up of a series of such steps? Is the departure from every rendezvous along the way made through such portals? I wonder if the passes function to orient the bird as it starts its evening journey northward. Clearly the Delta transients have not set their course until the pass is reached. Yet moving from the pass out over Lake Manitoba, their direction of flight, the same every year, is established.

Duck passes are not confined to the lakeshore. These are the doorways to the North. But the Marsh itself is a pattern of aerial trails as well marked by the lines of flight as is a state highway map. Resident ducks follow these trails almost as closely as mammals do their forest pathways. Such marsh travel invariably follows the line of least resistance; that is, the trails follow the shortest possible routes overland and avoid land travel wherever possible. Thus the pass is at the point of easiest connection between two bodies of water. Water areas are connected by a gap, channel, or creek, which are the passes.

In the absence of such waterways, the pass is at the narrowest neck of land separating the two areas, or along a dry creek that was once the connection. Where a waterway is long and winding, but the neck of land thin, the narrows rather than the water route is favored.

Since the marsh is a maze of scattered potholes, sloughs, and bays, a flight of any distance must take a duck over a number of passes. Young ducks or birds new to an area probably learn these passes through experience, selecting the natural crossings automatically, just as a fullback carries the ball through a hole that suddenly appears in his line. Or the crossings are learned through association with birds already familiar with the terrain. It is clear that the passes are familiar to resident birds. When a band is flushed it often is seen to fly directly toward a pass that is not yet within its vision.

The lakeshore passes, being portals to the lake, are used regardless of weather. But many of the marsh passes are used only in certain winds. A pass may be heavily used when the wind blows from the northwest or from the southeast, but seldom or never used in an east or west wind. Then crossing is made at another point. Thus, in its travel over the marsh, a duck has several trailways that are selected according to the wind. For example, one afternoon I stood at a narrow neck of land separating two large bays. About 3 p.m. a flight of canvasbacks moved over the pass in a continuous stream until dusk. The wind was slightly south of west. The birds came out of the northeast, alighting in the west bay to feed on abundant stands of sago pondweed. Next evening I returned to the narrows, but the wind had shifted, and although I remained

until dusk, no birds crossed. As I paddled home I found the west bay again abundant with canvasbacks which apparently had arrived by another route.

Some of the Marsh passes are very narrow. The flight of canvasbacks I saw confined its crossing to a span that was hardly more than thirty yards wide. At another pass I seldom saw the line of flight more than twenty yards wide, the width of the waterway. At still another pass near my cottage I seldom see the birds crossing more than ten yards either side of the lane's heart.

The same Marsh passes are used by all species of ducks. Some passes are used more frequently by one species than by others. This, I believe, is simply because different species go to different places to feed. Canvasbacks that loaf during the day on Cadham Bay fly east to their feeding waters over a route that is seldom followed by mallards. Mallards crossing to stubble follow trails that are used infrequently by canvasbacks. Several passes are heavily used only in late autumn when the lesser scaups crowd the Marsh.

Human activity does not seem to influence the movement over the passes. Hunters still take their bags at passes that their fathers shot over years ago. One of the most heavily used passes is directly over the village of Delta. Another crosses a highway. However, where a highway and its inevitable telephone line travel a narrows, many birds are killed by flying into the wires.

Man-made changes in terrain or vegetation sometimes influence travel. Where a pass crossed the lakeshore of woodland, it was believed that the lane might be more heavily used if a trough through the woods were created by clearing away the vegetation. All trees and shrubs were removed fifty yards either side of the lane's way, but following this clearing the ducks discontinued their use of the

left   Sunrise with ducks, Quill Lake, Saskatchewan. Kodachrome 64. f2.8 @ 250 sec. 35mm elmarit lens, Leica R4 camera.

pass and have never since crossed at that point.

The pass, of course, is but a step in a trail. In general, traffic from one pass to another follows well defined routes. Where ducks cross a large body of open water as they move from one pass to another, the line of flight usually is straight and direct over the water area. Also, when flight carries the bird any distance overland the movement is direct. When the terrain is broken by outstanding landmarks, the movement may be influenced by these. Thus, in their nightly movements to stubble, many mallards fly directly from their lakeshore passes to the fields. But one line of flight I watched was bent sharply. Investigation showed that the birds crossed the marsh following a dry creek bed which they followed to its end, thence moved to stubble.

Where a water area is broken by an undulating shoreline or by islands, the trails may digress according to the terrain. Travel frequently follows shorelines, swinging around rather than across points of land. Or, when the shoreline is much broken, the trail moves from point to point. The main travel does not cross over islands but follows the waterways between them. Flights frequently swing close to a lone island standing in an open sweep of water as though the birds must check their bearings at an important landmark.

The height at which a bird flies has much influence on its course of travel. In their local movements about the Marsh, ducks generally fly within fifty yards of the water. At such levels they follow the landmarks. When they fly at greater heights their movement is more direct. When flying low, a duck closely follows a water course or shoreline in all its meanderings. However, when moving high, although ducks follow the general course of creek or shore, the line of flight cuts corners and does not wind as the creek does.

This system of trails and passageways is evidence that a duck reacts positively to its environment, that it learns its position within its portion of world, and that the terrain once learned is remembered. To man, who tediously plods the earth, it seems incongruous that a duck, free in the boundless prairie skies, confines

Migrant flock of Canada geese arriving in early evening sunset, Delta, Manitoba. *Kodachrome 64. f4 @ 500 sec. 600mm/f-4 Nikkor super telephoto lens, Nikon F-4 camera.*

its movements to special trails. Yet without trails or landmarks in this flat prairie country, both man and ducks are lost. The pattern of aerial trails seems logical when we find ourselves, more often than not, independently following the same marshland travel paths and passes. I was astounded when I realized that any marshland travel I make, whether afoot on winter ice or by canoe in summer, parallels many ducks' trails. The canoe trail from the Station landing to the bay three miles east follows in all its details the most important duck lane between two points.

Ducks are not the only birds with special lanes at Delta. For some species the lakeshore is not crossed, but is itself a lane of travel. These migrant birds meet at the east corner of Lake Manitoba, follow the shoreline westward to the west shore, thence move again cross-country into the northwest. But I have never seen a duck hawk following the shoreline. Instead, this species strikes out over the lake. Blackbirds of all species follow the lakeshore, invariably moving along a strip of marshland just behind the shoreline

border of woods. For several days in spring there is an endless stream of blackbirds flying west, until one wonders if all their worldly numbers are passing in parade. Crows as well as blue jays follow the lakeshore westward in their spring movements. Among the remainder of the passerines I know of none that follow special lanes. Their great abundance along every portion of the lake ridge during migration, and the absence of any conspicuous east-west movement suggest that they probably fly out over the lake in a broad sweep when they depart. I have also seen snow buntings moving straight out over the lake on northward passage. The aerial trails of all birds are fascinating to follow.

Although structurally adapted for life in an aquatic environment, ducks are not completely independent of land forms. Many species nest on land, most loaf on land during some period of their daily or seasonal routine, and some feed on land during certain seasons.

Land forms provide loafing sites which are an important part of any waterfowl breeding marsh. As well as muskrat houses and matted reeds, the most important loafing sites are on the exposed earth of shorelines. In general, acceptable loafing spots are free of growing vegetation and occur in many locations.

One favorite spot is the grazed shoreline. On the sandy lakeshore, broad sections of beach have been completely denuded of plant growth by grazing cattle. Such open beach is heavily used by loafing bands of drakes in late May and June prior to the flightless season. It is preferred over ungrazed shoreline where vegetation reaches to the water edge, or open sand bars, which are exposed in summer and flooded. In the Marsh itself small areas of shoreline have also been grazed clean of cover and are used by loafing birds. Populations of cattle that are numerous enough to graze a shoreline in marshlands, also overgraze nesting cover to the extent that such marsh is inferior for nesting populations. Even populations of cattle that are too small to overgraze nesting cover nevertheless create some shoreline areas that are trodden bare of cover where they move to the marsh edge for water. In fact, portions of the Delta ditch where cattle gathering to drink have trodden a narrow strip of ditch-side barren of cover are used heavily by summering drakes.

Small muskrat slides along the Delta ditch and mud bars formed by declining water levels in summer also provide loafing spots for territorial pairs and are used by summering drakes and autumn transients. The mid-summer decline of water levels exposes sand bars along the lakeshore that are heavily used by the stubble mallards. However, such bars are not available when flooded by wind tides due to a north wind.

Sunset/storm clouds. Kodachrome 64. f2.8 @ 250 sec. 35mm elmarit lens, Leica R4 camera.

72

Windrows of plant material, loosened by ice or wave action or cut by muskrats, are washed ashore sometimes in such quantities that they retard shoreline vegetation sufficiently to provide temporary loafing sites for ducks. In late summer muskrats sometimes cut away bulrushes, providing open patches of shallow water which are also attractive as loafing sites. Boulders that protrude above the water level are also used as loafing spots by territorial pairs if the boundaries are near the shoreline. There are few boulders in Delta Marsh, but in some Manitoba areas boulders are frequent enough to be important territorial loafing sites.

Muskrat house, Ventura Marsh, Iowa. *Kodachrome 64. f8 @ 250 sec. 180mm apo-telyt-r lens, Leica R4 camera.*

Land is no barrier to broods of flightless young. How far broods can travel overland is an important and still unanswered question in management, for the success of ducklings reared in small potholes depends upon finding a permanent water area within brood walking distance of the smaller, early drying waters. At Delta, broods have been observed to travel overland five miles and it is inferred that some broods travel as far as eight miles between one water area and another.

Flightless adults move short distances inland through heavy cover in escape movements. Mallards and pintails, and to a lesser extent a few other species of river ducks, regularly take to land to feed on agricultural crops. Such departures from water generally are of short duration. Passage to and from the feeding areas is by flight.

Northern shoveler hen on muskrat house, Quill Lake, Sasktachewan. *Kodachrome 64. f8 @ 250 sec. 135mm elmarit lens, Leica R4 camera.*

The soil of marsh bottoms is another consideration. In an area as heavily shot over by hunters as Delta Marsh is in the autumn open season, the nature of the soil underlying the marsh is important. Some of the most used feeding beds are in this area. At some points that have been used as shooting stands for at least three generations of gunners, the lead deposited in the marsh bottom must amount to several tons. If the marsh had a hard bottom much of this shot would be available to ducks since they require gravel for the digestion of their food and might eat the shot accidentally or mistake it for grit. Although gravel underlines the silt bottom in many parts of the Marsh, it is generally covered by a heavy layer of bottom soil and the lead shots sink into this soft muck and little is available to feeding birds.

Much of the gravel that ducks require is obtained on the lakeshore or along the paths, trails, and roads traversing the marsh edge. Some is exposed at canoe landings, at cattle watering spots, and in a few areas within the Marsh where there is gravel bottom. Ducks require land, as long as it is suitable for their needs and near water.

p76   Habitat/bulrush marsh, Alexander Griswold Marsh, Manitoba. *Kodachrome 64. f8 @ 250 sec. 50mm summicron lens, Leica R6 camera.*

Canvasback brood loafing on log, Minnedosa, Manitoba. *Kodachrome 64. f6.3 @ 250 sec. 280mm apo-telyt-r lens, Leica R4 camera.*

75

Ducks may spend part of their daily routine on land, but it is a truism that land without water is duckless. Across the North American continent the distribution of ducks is patterned by the distribution of water areas. Not all waters, however, are equally attractive to ducks. On the breeding grounds their use of a water area depends upon the size, shape, and depth of water bodies, the chemical and physical properties, and the currents.

There is an important relationship between the size of a water area and its acceptability to breeding ducks. In general small water areas are superior to large waters. Wind tides have a lot to do with the choice. Large bodies of water are subject to variations in water level because of these tides, which sometimes are severe. At the south end of Lake Manitoba, for example, as on other large Manitoba lakes, all loafing areas may be obliterated by rising waters during periods of north wind. Sometimes loafing areas are under water for days at a time. Summering drakes and stubble birds are tolerant of such changes, moving elsewhere for the period of the storm. Territorial pairs, however, are less tolerant of flooded loafing spots, and flooding is more severe and of longer duration during the spring period of territorial occupancy than later in the season when the females aren't nesting.

Wave action accompanying onshore winds and the exposed beaches of offshore winds limit the distribution of shoreline aquatic plants because the stands of emergent vegetation are periodically subjected to floods or exposure. Thus, on large bodies of water not only are the loafing areas unstable, but the shoreline food supply is scarce and nesting cover is second-rate. All of these factors tend to limit the distribution of territorial pairs on exposed shorelines of large bodies of water.

The inferiority of such shorelines is shown in a comparison with marsh shorelines. In 1942 Cadham Bay, within Delta Marsh, held thirty-six territorial pairs per mile of shoreline. The lakeshore averaged nine pairs per mile for the same period. The marsh accommodated many water-nesting species; the lakeshore accommodated none, which was probably due to the frequent exposure and flooding of the vegetation.

Wind tides, of course, cause variations of water levels in marshes as well, when, like Delta Marsh, they are fed by lake waters. Where only a few channels feed an extensive system of bays, however, variations in water level are much more gradual than on the lake. On Delta Marsh, rising water levels, except in the most severe and prolonged storms, rise so gradually that they permit many nesting hens to build their nests above the flood. On the Netley Marsh at the southern end of Lake Winnipeg, however, the wind tides annually cause severe destruction of redhead nests. The pattern of bays at Netley differs from the Delta pattern. Some isolated bays are fed directly by channels from Lake Winnipeg or the Red River and rising waters are much more severe than at Delta.

Within Delta Marsh several of the larger bays are subject to local wind tides and severe wave action. Prevailing winds during the nesting season are from the northwest. In the large bays, territorial pairs are less common and nesting among the water-nesting species is less successful along southern shorelines that

receive the force of local tide and wave action. Besides the action of wind on water, wind itself may limit the distribution of territorial pairs. In small water areas the force of wind is broken by vegetation, or the pairs may seek escape from the wind by entering shoreline vegetation during severe blows. On the exposed lakeshore, however, there is no escape from wind except in departure elsewhere to sheltered sites. Not only is the shoreline of large water areas rendered inferior to territorial pairs by the action

above Bluebills, courtship flight. *Kodachrome 64. f4 @ 500 sec. 600mm/f-4 Nikkor super telephoto lens, Nikon F-3 camera.*

right Mallard pair resting, Ventura Marsh, Iowa. *Kodachrome 64. f5.6 @ 250 sec. 280mm apo-telyt-r lens, Leica R6 camera.*

far right Cattail marsh, Delta, Manitoba. *Koda-chrome 64. f11 @ 250 sec. 19mm fisheye lens, Leica R6 camera.*

80

of wind and water but, in proportion to water acreage, shorelines of large areas are relatively shorter than shorelines of smaller water. All other things being equal, the length of shoreline in proportion to water acreage decreases as the size of the water area increases. In simple geometric design, an area five miles square has a border of twenty miles, or one mile of border for every eight hundred acres enclosed. But in separate units each of one square mile, the same area of enclosure is bounded by one hundred miles of border or one mile of border for every one hundred and sixty acres enclosed. In terms of water and shoreline, it will be seen that many

small areas with their greater total shoreline can accommodate more territorial pairs than a single large area.

The size of the area is conditioned by its shape. Logan Bennett, who first pointed to the importance of shoreline in the distribution of nesting waterfowl,[11] demonstrated that shape as well as size of water area influences the length of usable margins. An area one mile wide and ten miles long has a shoreline of twenty-two miles, while another area of the same water acreage a half mile wide and twenty miles long has a shoreline of forty-one miles. There is no doubt that contours influence length of shoreline. An area with many points and bays has a greater shoreline than one with an even margin. Islands likewise increase the total shoreline.

Ice is another factor that must be considered. Small bodies of water are free of ice earlier in spring than are large areas. At Delta the first ice-free waters are the sloughs and potholes, then the smaller bays, then the larger bays, and finally the lake. The smaller areas are available to spring migrants and to territorial pairs earlier than the large areas. This difference in timing may be short or long depending upon the severity of the winter and the nature of the thaw. The importance of water with shoreline early in the spring cannot be overstated. Territorial pairs need these sites for successful nesting.

In the honeysuckle by my gate a catbird sings his throat out; from the top of the old willow comes a robin's carol; and from the lower shrubs come the ragtime tunes of my yellow warbler, song sparrow, and house wren. Suddenly, from down the lane comes the twitter of kingbirds. The songsters cease their outbursts abruptly and I see my yellow warbler dart quickly into the heart of the lilac. I know the reason for the quiet even before I look up to see a marsh hawk swing by with the kingbirds darting at his back. He pays little attention to his diminutive pursuers; nevertheless, he leaves my neighborhood and sails out over the meadow. The kingbirds return triumphantly to their cherry tree; the yellow warbler peeks out from behind a lilac leaf; and in a moment my birds are in full chorus again.

Yellow-headed blackbird, Minnedosa, Manitoba. Ektachrome 100. f5.6 @ 250 sec. 280mm apo-telyt-r lens, Leica R4 camera.

From my porch I watch the hawk sail low over the grassy lea. Then, as he approaches a patch of cattails near the slough, a band of yellow-headed blackbirds rises in a body, hanging over the harrier, swooping at him like spitfires, giving voice all the while to their harsh call. The hawk twists and darts among their company, then drops out of sight for a moment behind the rushes. When he lifts into the air again, the angry birds dive all the harder at him, for in his talons he has one of their nestlings. Soon, however, he is far away with his tender meal, and the blackbirds, forgetful of his aggression, settle back to their own busy doings about the slough.

From my doorstep to the farthest corners of our planet, the world of animals is in constant, non-ceasing conflict. The average citizen, no matter how deep within the walls of civilization he may be, can witness daily examples of this battle for life. Every neighborhood has its cats and house sparrows; and the age-old aggression of one upon the other may be seen by the most casual observer at least once or twice a year. Much of our folklore and the bedtime stories of our childhood play upon the events of this constant battle for life: the story of the fox and the hare, the cat and the mouse, the wolf and the stag are known by children of every generation.

This battle for life in the animal world takes place every minute of every day wherever blood pounds through hearts. It is, indeed, one of the fundamental beats of the pulse of life itself. Everywhere, in daylight or in darkness, in forests or in meadows, on mountain tops or deep within the sea, all living creatures are alert to this battle. Some try to sustain life through evasion from those that hunt them, while the hunters are constantly trying to sustain their lives by the food they must obtain through the pursuit. For all animal life on this earth this conflict between one kind and another is as deep-seated as the irresistible urge for reproduction.

The battle for life in the animal world is distinguished from all other types of combat by the fact that the victor eats the vanquished. Characteristically, too, the combat is between two widely divergent types of animals. Rarely, except under abnormal or artificial conditions, does it take place between members of the same kind.

I can witness this battle for life in my own garden. There seem to be basic rules. Take, for example, the most conspicuous members of this small animal community, the birds of the passerine order which include the familiar songsters. Here, members of a given species do not engage each other in this type of combat. Robins do not kill and eat other robins, nor do catbirds eat catbirds, nor does my yellow warbler make a meal of his neighbor two hedgerows down the lane.

Dividing this particular order into its specific groups, however, I find that there is some aggression of one species upon the other. By and large such conflict consists of an attack by an adult of one species upon the young or eggs of another. The bronzed grackle sometimes eats the eggs or young of the yellow warbler, while the crow and the blue jay, both members of the songsters order, are notorious nest robbers. Yet the numbers of birds preying upon close relatives is comparatively small and there is only one species of this order, the shrike, that regularly kills and eats adults of other songbirds.

Beyond the borders of close relationship, however, there is severe and universal aggression. The members of the hawk tribe all prey upon the songbirds. The songbirds themselves feed abundantly upon lower animal forms, principally insects. In other groups of animals it is much the same. Wolves eat rabbits, deer, cattle, and many other forms of flesh; Cooper's hawks and bald eagles, foxes and coyotes, mink and weasels all live wholly or partially upon animal flesh, but each species does not normally live upon the flesh of its own kind.

Not only does this conflict for flesh take place between animals of different kinds, but invariably it occurs between a strong, efficient aggressor, whose physical make-up magnificently equips it for killing, and a weaker, generally smaller prey species whose only defense is evasion. With birds the heaviest aggressions for food are made upon insects and other invertebrates. The spoonbill duck preys upon innumerable small aquatic organisms, but is itself preyed upon by hawks. Fish are the principal food for many birds and mammals, all of which are in some manner specially adapted for the pursuit and killing of the finny tribe. In the mammal world the rabbit, mouse, and deer are the legendary prey of all meat-eaters.

Some animals find themselves at the bottom of the scale, being preyed upon, but not eating flesh themselves. These are the vegetarians. Many insects and other invertebrates fall into this class. In large measure most of our rodents, as well as deer and cattle, are vegetarians, although some will eat flesh when the occasion presents.

Peregrine falcon (duck hawk) in flight. *Kodachrome film, telephoto lens, Minolta 35mm camera. Complete technical data is unavailable.*

87

A very few species, notably the wolf, lion, and eagle, are at the very top of the pyramid, killing many other forms for food but not offering themselves as food for other flesh-eaters. The battle for life is really a chain by which the plant world provides food for all animal life. The vegetarian obtains its life spark directly from plants, passing vegetation on to others in the form of flesh and blood. Sometimes this chain may be short: willow bark, snowshoe hare, red fox. Or is may have several links: potato, potato bug, rose-breasted grosbeak, sharp-shinned hawk.

While the drive of this battle is ever downward, with the strong killing the weak, nature has given the oppressed species a defense in numbers. This is apparent in any garden when we compare the number of angleworms with robins. Insects outnumber songbirds many fold; songbirds greatly outnumber hawks. The ability of the rabbit to increase its numbers is of legendary humor, and it is an established fact that where foxes and rabbits live, the latter greatly outnumber the former.

Conflict holds the world in delicate balance and we do not have to look far to see what happens when this balance is not in operation. Some years ago, for instance, professional hunters and trappers all but rid Arizona's Kaibab Forest of mountain lion. The native deer, with no natural force to hold them in check, increased to such tremendous numbers that they devoured their own food supply and were reduced to starvation. And any schoolboy knows how the gulls came to rid the Mormons of their grasshopper plague. Without birds to prey upon them, insects would make this a sorry world.

Once a year our society sets aside a week to think and plan for the well-being of the fish, birds, and mammals that make up such an important portion of the natural wealth of our land. To a large group of us, wildlife has purely aesthetic values, measured in terms of the pleasures and beauties brightening our lives whenever we come in contact with our wild neighbors. For others there is added to this aesthetic return, the material values of the hunt, when our wildlife provides us with food as well as recreation. Both of these have economic values for our society that can be measured in dollars and cents.

Yet there is another value that is more difficult to describe. Our wildlife is but a part of the complex make-up of our land, just as leaves are a part of the forest. While these wild things live with us their presence is visual evidence that we humans are still in harmony with our environment. When our human abuse of the land is such that native wildlife does not thrive, we should know that we have upset the natural balance of our land in such a manner that we, its human occupants, will eventually suffer. The condition of our wildlife is a barometer of our advance along the road of civilization. Thus the master plan for conservation of wildlife is just as important to those city dwellers who may be unaware of its existence, as it is to hunter, trapper, or garden bird-lover.

It is more than a generation since Hewitt and Taverner and Audubon and other great naturalists began the crusade for conservation. Much has been accomplished since their time, particulary in the field of scientific wildlife management. This science had its real beginning in the 1920s. It grows and develops slowly; yet, wherever science has been given the guiding hand, we are measuring the visual, material, and economic returns of a healthier environment and more abundant wildlife populations.

The development of science in wildlife is slow. It has two great obstacles. The first is public objection. This is understandable. Hunters and trappers often feel that they, the sons of the land, are the true experts on wildlife management. They resent the intrusion of the scientific outlook which they do not understand. It is a strange anomaly that many men who practise science in their

Oak Hammock Marsh, Manitoba. *Kodachrome 64. f8 @ 250 sec. 50mm summicron lens, Leica R4 camera.*

90

own professions, often resent the intrusion of science in wildlife management. Yet a scientific approach that is dictated by precise and careful examination of the wildlife population under study has the objective to restore wildlife resources to a position they once occupied. The first move in stepping up production of a depleted species is understanding why the species is declining. If people want to continue to enjoy the wildlife population, a scientific study of wildlife future well-being is necessary.

The second major obstacle is political apathy. This has confronted all scientific programs since the beginning of science. It can be overcome only by deliberate, patient demonstration and education. We cannot expect to make headway in our management of wildlife until our leaders are sympathetic to the values of science. These two obstacles can be overcome together; for when the people have measured the values of science, so will politicians respond in action for science.

Universities have a responsibility here. It is not simply the university function to train a small number of specialists or to undertake biological research. They must bring the aesthetic and economic values of wildlife into the overall academic plan. The student of engineering, agriculture, law, or architecture whose program has included at least an orientation course in conservation, and who has associated with other students and professors who are daily concerned with the problems of conservation, is a better and more caring citizen when he takes his place in the world. Where such orientation courses exist, as at Cornell or Wisconsin, they are not only popular, but have a measured influence in broadened outlooks. The advancement of many conservation programs so often depends upon the sympathetic understanding of an engineer, architect,

above   Blue-winged teal on nest/prairie lilies, Minnedosa, Manitoba. *Kodachrome 64. f6.3 @ 250 sec. 135mm elmarit lens, Leica R4 camera.*

left   Mallard flock, Lake Manitoba marshes. *Kodachrome 64. f4 @ 500 sec. 600mm/f-4 Nikkor super telephoto lens, Nikon F-4 camera.*

93

or agriculturist who has some background of understanding in natural history. In the early years of civilization our culture in many ways was built from our associations with the wild things about us. Now, as our lives become more and more distant from nature, it is important that we keep in touch with the other occupants of our land.

With respect to the management of our migratory waterfowl, the rapid advancement of knowledge is due to the scientific approach—the cause-and-effect experiments and investigations into the dynamics of wildfowl populations. However, even this expansion of our knowledge has not provided all the answers and truths we seek. Waterfowl are still in dangerously low numbers. The situation is serious with the duck population. Until the general public and administrators reach some common understanding with regard to our waterfowl population and the need for scientific management of this resource, the future of wildfowl, especially ducks, is in hazard.

Bluebills flight, Lake
Manitoba marshes.
*Kodachrome 64. f4 @
500 sec. 600mm/f-4 Nikkor
super telephoto lens, Nikon
F-3 camera.*

In the shrubby borders of my yard, and in the tangle of willows beyond, there lives throughout the year a small population of snowshoe hares, white as snow in winter, piebald in spring and fall, and forest gray in summer. Of all the beasts that frequent my neighborhood, the snowshoe is the most timid. He is more timid than the little white-footed mouse who will bite my finger if I capture him in the corner of the woodshed. Hunted by all the flesh-eaters, and subsisting only on vegetation, this bunny hides all day, venturing forth only with the dropping of nightfall. I know him only by an occasional fleeting shadow across my lawn at twilight or by the lacework of trails he leaves upon the winter snows.

Annually, in the month of April when the mating instinct surges within them, the males of this timid clan venture forth to engage each other in bitter duels. Bright spring mornings when I step out into the lane to catch the voice of some songbird newly arrived from the South, I find a patch of earth and sod torn asunder by the snowshoes' nightly tussle. Scattered here and there are tufts of fur, sometimes clinging to great patches of torn skin, and the sand is sprinkled with blood.

With all our mammals and birds, no matter how docile or timid, or weak or small, the time of the taking of a mate is a period of combat. Such combat, as distinguished from the battle of life, is always between members of the same kind: hare fights hare, fox fights fox, and duck fights duck and goose fights goose for the choice of a mate. The object of the combat is not food but the mate, and the victor does not normally eat the vanquished. Such combat is among the males in all species except a few, such as the phalarope, in which the mating role is exchanged and the female plays a dominant role.

left   Canada geese and mallards, Delta, Manitoba. *Kodachrome 64. f4 @ 500 sec. 600mm/f-4 Nikkor super telephoto lens, Nikon F-4 camera.*

below   Northern shovelers in flight, Delta, Manitoba. *Kodachrome 200. f8 @ 500 sec. 280mm apo-telyt-r lens, Leica R4 camera.*

There are many types of such prenuptial combat and many species are highly specialized for such fighting. The bull elk has well developed antlers and the members of the sheep tribe have horns with which to combat each other. In many gallinaceous birds, which include our common poultry, the males have well developed spurs for fighting. Some shorebirds and geese have spurs upon the wings.

In the deer where the antlers are found primarily in the male, the specialized nature of the use of these weapons for sexual fighting and not for defense against predator, is shown by the fact that the antlers are dropped shortly after the mating season. With species that have no special tools for fighting, the combat at mating time is no less severe. Many songbirds and waterfowl, for example, engage in fights which, though they may be short, are fearsome duels.

A few animals fight to the death. Frequently in the case of deer with locked antlers, both contestants die. Generally, however, the vanquished one gives up and departs from the field of battle before he receives a mortal wound. With birds living in their elastic wild environment, and being highly mobile creatures, the combats are generally brief, the weaker individual usually retiring from the advances of the strong before receiving severe bodily harm. However, within the inelastic confines of captivity these sexual fights not infrequently end in death to the vanquished who cannot escape from the victor. In the many fights I have witnessed among ducks in the wild I have never seen one contestant severely injured by the other, but there have been frequent deaths in combat among the ducks I hold in captivity.

In most species of birds and mammals the fight for the possession of the mate is an annual affair. Wild animals, unlike humans or domestic poultry, live a new life cycle each year. In the autumn they are sexless, senile beings incapable of reproduction. With the onset of spring their reproductive organs develop until they seek, first to obtain a mate, then to establish a home and rear the young. With the coming of autumn again the reproductive organs regress, and they are sexless beings again. In some mammals the period of sexual activity, of fighting and mating, takes place in the autumn. This is true of the members of our deer and their autumn rutting period is known to all woodsmen.

When the short annual period of courting and mating is over, the males of most species depart from their mates. When the season for love again returns the males must court and fight once more for the right to a female. This period of combat takes up only a small portion of each year.

far right   Mallards feeding, Dalton, Missouri. *Kodachrome 64. f5.6 @ 250 sec. 135mm elmarit lens, Leica R6 camera.*

98

In domestic species, however, in which man through domestication has induced the courtship cycle to remain at its peak throughout most or all of the year, fighting may take place at any time. This is true in poultry. The game cock in the pit is not fighting for his master's money but to conquer a sexual opponent.

With early man the winning of a mate probably was much the same as in the animal world. The strong vanquished the weak in severe, brutal combat for the right to a female. Today, the cloak of civilization has robbed most of us of the chance to enter into bitter combat for the hand of a lady. Yet many of our athletic contests, which occupy such an important place in our national life, have survived from the past. Who is there to say that the prowess of the male on the athletic field does not have some bearing when the lady makes her final choice.

Athletic combat, as with the agressive behavior of courting, is a universal characteristic of males the world over. Attendance at athletic events is partly to see the team win, partly, as anyone knows who has watched a crowd at an exciting game, to enter personally into the contest by proxy. When, in the old days Babe Ruth stepped up to the plate, he was not Babe Ruth alone, but a thousand men who, tense in the stands, themselves knocked the ball over the fence. Likewise when a twentieth-century male who never did anything more strenuous than carry out the garbage and has never been in a scrap since the fourth grade, sits in a darkened theater and watches the hero fight the villian, he flexes his own muscles and, with one swift blow by proxy, sends the opponent to the dust.

Northern pintails and ring-billed gulls, Quill Lake, Saskatchewan. *Kodachrome 64. f11 @ 500 sec. 90mm summicron lens, Leica R4 camera.*

Every man, sometime in his life, seeks the wilderness. Usually that for which he searches is quite intangible; it is a deep-seated and compelling need, yet he knows not where to find it. Does it exist in the quiet of a city street before dawn, or in the melody of a lark's song? A country lane at twilight, the prow of a ship at sea, the silent vastness of a great cathedral, or the hush and grandeur of a pristine forest may provide the setting.

However the individual defines wilderness and wherever he finds it, he realizes that experiencing it is a thing vital to him and to all mankind. For that which impels man to seek the wilderness is a searching restlessness within the soul. And that which is sought is not the physical wilderness itself, but the isolation that allows him to contemplate his goals and ideals. He pursues a truth that is found only through his communication with something greater than himself. The longing is for the truth of his being, the search to confirm that he is not merely flesh, but something more; that he is part of the inspiration of the universe. For most men, wilderness provides the inner peace to sate the restlessness. If men regularly commune with wilderness, they bring from it truths that shape their lives forever. Within the wilderness of the cathedral Galileo found the truth of gravity. In the wilderness of the Atlantic, Columbus found the truth of America and the shape of the world. In the wilderness of a petri dish, Fleming found the truth of penicillin, and in the wilderness of the Northwest, Lewis and Clark found the truth of our great land.

For me, wilderness is the great outdoors. I find peace in the harmony that exists in nature and I seek the unspoiled land and its wild creatures to renew my spirit. I know that many people feel as I do. It is important to keep some areas of our land free from cultivation and the intrusion of civilization. It is important that man has a place of retreat when the cares of life and the confines of urban society weigh heavily upon him. Anyone who has spent a Sunday in a metropolitan park or a July at Yellowstone knows how widespread is this need to find in nature a place of solace for the spirit.

After the Civil War and after World War I we wastefully despoiled much of the

p104 Sunset, Big Grass Marsh, Manitoba. *Kodachrome 64. f4 @ 250 sec. 50mm summicron lens, Leica R4 camera.*

p105 Mallards and blue-winged teal, sunrise, Ponas Heritage Marsh, Saskatchewan. *Kodachrome 64. f2.8 @ 250 sec. 50mm summicron lens, Leica R4 camera.*

103

land in our haste to reap its rich resources. Gradually we have learned the values of conservation of soil, water, forest, and wildlife, so that within the boundaries of our own land there is hope that we may not again see the greatest waste. In our hurry to progress we must not pillage the land. Let us take heed of the lessons of the past and take care, individually and nationally, that we do not spoil the wild areas for present and future generations.

Within our own land there still exists some unbroken wild places that serve humanity best in their natural state. It is our obligation to preserve these wilderness lands that are still left within our borders. We are a vigorous strong nation, more so now than ever before. But if the time comes when our ordinary citizens can find no space to hear the song of the pine trees, or wonder at the beauty of unscarred mountains, or start at the far-off howl of the wolf, then we will lose the best part of ourselves and our country will not prosper.

Female gadwall on nest with young, Delta, Manitoba. *Kodachrome 64. f8 @ 250 sec. 90mm summicron lens, Leica R4 camera.*

Saturday night! For those of us who live in the country this is the big event of the week: early supper, hurry with the dishes, a change into the best clothes, and off to town for three hours of shopping and gossip. This night Joan and I were heading across the Marsh at sunset for Portage la Prairie, Manitoba, eighteen miles away. We had just slipped through Slack's Bluff on the far side of the Marsh when Joan, who always sees things first, touched my arm and I pulled the car to a stop. "There, over Portage Creek. What are they, ducks or geese?"

Far to the southeast a thin line hung above the horizon, a wisp of a thread barely visible. We watched in silence as it grew. It approached rapidly and soon we could make out its component. "Geese!" All of a sudden their voices drifted to us. "Wavies!" We stepped from the car and stood in the gathering dusk to watch them pass. Most of them were dark—the blue goose. But their lines were punctuated here and there by singles, twos, or threes of white birds with black primaries—the lesser snow goose. Both species are widely known as "wavies." They flew in a great wide line from which spread many smaller lines, the whole forming a great round-pointed "V." As it moved, the mass of birds rose and fell as if riding on a rolling swell. Individuals within the mass constantly shifted their positions in the lines, so that the pattern of the flock was changing constantly. The birds were in full and constant voice. Their low gabble was by no means as exciting as the whoop of swans or the bark of the Canada goose, but nevertheless, it made sweet music over the April prairie.

The birds held steady course. Then at a point above Slack's Bluff, they turned sharply to the west. As their voices faded there came a louder clang from the east. Almost upon us was another band. From as far as we could see the geese came, one great line after the other, each spaced a mile or so apart.

right   Canada geese, Lake Manitoba marshes. *Kodachrome 64. f4 @ 500 sec. 600mm/f-4 Nikkor super telephoto lens, Nikon F-3 camera.*

far right   Snow and blue geese spring migration, Delta, Manitoba. *Kodachrome 64. f4 @ 500 sec. 600mm/f-4 Nikkor super telephoto lens, Nikon F-3 camera.*

108

I shall make no attempt to express here the unbounded feeling of joy that was in our hearts as we watched those battalions as they passed, nor attempt to picture the beauty of the scene. It was one of the great moments of my life and for some reason I could not suppress the urge to take off my hat until the last group had passed before our review.

It is clear that these birds knew where they were going. After stopping at Delta for several weeks they left again to fly northeast to James Bay, hence northward to their Arctic breeding grounds. We who are men wonder how they travel this uncharted course that we could not follow without delicate instruments. Yet the turning at Slack's Bluff makes me wonder if indeed their course is charted, but by a knowledge beyond ours.

REFERENCES

1. J. Fenimore Cooper, *The Prairie*. D. Appletons & Company, New York, 1873.
2. *Webster's Dictionary*, 1964 edition.
3. G. E. Hutchinson, *Treatise on Limnology*, Vol. 1. Wiley, 1966.
4. J. G. Needham and J. T. Lloyd, *Life of Inland Waters*, 3rd ed. Comstock 1937.
5. R. L. Smith, *Ecology in Field Biology*, Harper & Row, 1966.
6. J. H. Zumberge, *The Lakes of Minnesota, Their Origin and Classification*, University of Minnesota Press, 1952.
7. L. K. Sowls, "A Preliminary Report on Renesting in Waterfowl," in *Transactions of the North American Wildlife Conference*. 14:260–273, 1949.
8. M. Milowski, "The Significance of Farmland for Waterfowl Nesting & Techniques for Reducing Losses to Agricultural Practices" in *Transactions of the North American Wildlife Conference* 23:215–228, 1958.
9. P. H. Klopfer, "An Analyses of Learning in Young Anatidea," *Ecology*. 40:90–102, 1957.
10. E. R. Kalmbach, 1939 "Nesting success. A Significance in Waterfowl Reproduction," *Transactions of the North American Wildlife Conference*, 4:595–604, 1939. P. L. Errington, 1942 "On the Analogies of Productivity in Populations of Higher Vertebrates," *Journal of Wildlife Management*, 6(2):165–181. B. W. Cartwright, 1952 "A comparison of Potential with Actual Waterfowl Production." *Transactions of the North American Wildlife Conference*, 17:131–137. L. K. Sowls, 1955 *Prairie Ducks*. Wildlife Management Institute, Washington D.C.
11. Logan J. Bennett, 1938 *Blue-winged Teal; Its Ecology and Management*. Collegiate Press, Ames, Iowa, 1938 and Bennett, "Duck Nesting Carrying Capacities in Iowa," *Transactions of the North American Wildlife Conference*, 1936.

PHOTOGRAPHING BIRDS IN FLIGHT

Jack Barrie's first and most important advice about successfully photographing waterfowl in flight is to know the habits and habitats of the birds. Canvasbacks, pintails, mallards all have distinctive traits that should be learned before ever attempting to photograph the birds. And he suggests that you work on only one species at a time. Jack usually studies the flight patterns of the subject bird for at least two weeks before a photo session and carefully chooses an ideal location where he knows wind and light conditions will be suitable.

His next advice is to have the right equipment. His main lens is a Nikon 600mm f/4 costing nearly $10,000. He takes most of his photographs at a shutter speed of 1/500 of a second, which he says gives depth of field and is usually fast enough for birds in flight. He finds that a shutter speed of 1/1000 of a second stops the action too much at the expense of critical depth of field. The shutter speed of 1/500 of a second is ideal, even for faster flying birds. He doesn't use filters much either, except a skylight filter for protection of the expensive front glass of the lens. All filters cut light and he is always wanting more light. Jack suggests that beginning photographers should start with a good quality 300mm f2.8 lens, along with a 1.4x and 2x teleconverter and a good quality 35mm Single Lens Reflex camera equipped with a motordrive. From the same blind you will be able to change to three different focal lengths (magnifications), depending on the distance of the ducks, all for less cost than the price of a longer lens.

Jack never photographs ducks and geese in early autumn because the marsh is still too green for a convincing autumn shot and the waterfowl do not have their best plumage. He prefers to shoot in early spring when for three weeks the marsh resembles fall and all the birds are colorful. Besides, at this time they are distracted by mating rituals and a photographer can ease his way closer for a good flight shot and witness some interesting courtship behavior as well.

Midday light is his preference because it defines true-colors. The soft tones of early morning and evening turn the cheek of the Canada goose an orange shade and muffle the detail of the feathers. Jack usually sets his camera for the reading he obtains when he points his lens at the marsh grass near the waterline and relies on this and the camera's built-in meter for his film exposure.

Panning and focusing skills to capture birds in flight were more difficult to develop. Jack practised by following cars along a busy overpass. This experience showed him that the heavy lens could not be handled smoothly. He and his wife experimented with brooms and string to tie him and the lens together. It worked so well that he had an aluminum bracket made and he is still using it. He uses his shoulders to do the panning, holding the electric shutter release in his right hand and focusing the lens with he left hand. The camera moves with his body and this is his secret which allows him to freeze a shot and get depth of field on fine-grain film.

PHOTOGRAPHING WILDFOWL IN HABITAT

Glenn Chambers believes that knowing your subject is the secret to good wildlife photography. Because he is a wildlife biologist he has in-depth knowledge about the characteristics and habits of the creatures he captures on film. This is important for all animals but is particularly beneficial when photographing nesting ducks which are easily frightened and can abandon nests which would contribute to the already low population of these birds. Glenn's main concern is the well-being of the photographic subject. When he wishes to photograph a female canvasback nest, for example, he first fences the area to keep away mammals such as mink, foxes, coyotes, skunks, which have learned to follow human scent to nests and destroy them. Glenn approaches the nest through the water so he won't leave a scent for predators to follow. He never approaches a nest after 3 pm and always watches and studies the hen for several days from a distance to learn when she will best tolerate his presence and equipment. The longer a hen sits on the nest the more broody she becomes and brooding hens are the most tolerant of slight disturbances. Usually the optimum time for good photographs is just before and during hatching of the young. Some of the best poses are secured at that time.

Glenn also builds a camouflaged blind. He places it 40 feet away from the nest and moves it several feet closer every day. His favorite blind that he uses on water is a floating hut made of styrofoam and canvas and covered with cattails and suitable vegetation. It looks like a muskrat house and it allows him to approach unsuspecting swimming and loafing ducks for some very good photographs.

He also uses a cocoon-like blind that he climbs into and lays flat on the ground for some photography. This works well for arctic-nesting ducks and geese who are used to the flat tundra and are suspicious of any change in the landscape.

Glenn uses a Leica R6 because of the superior quality of the optics in the lenses and a Minolta 9xi as a back-up camera because of the auto-focus feature. He cautions that the Minolta is sometimes frustrating, however, because the camera is designed so that it will not expose a frame unless the subject is in focus. Many good opportunities are missed because of this. He uses short telephoto lenses — 135mm in length is his favorite — for close-up photos once the blind is in the required position. His preference is Kodachrome 64 film. This is not a "fast" film but it gives great natural color. Another preference is Fujichrome Velvia exposed at ASA 40 instead of the suggested ASA 50. Under soft light conditions this film produces an excellent effect.

Glenn photographs all aspects of waterfowl behavior. He uses the studies to learn about the birds' life history and to sell to publishers.

INDEX

Photographs listed in italic.